BEST
AUSTRALIAN
COMEDY
WRITING

Published by Affirm Press in 2015
28 Thistlethwaite Street, South Melbourne, VIC 3205.
www.affirmpress.com.au

National Library of Australia Cataloguing-in-Publication entry
available for this title.
Title: Best Australian Comedy Writing / Edited by Luke Ryan
ISBN: 9781922213754 (paperback)

Cover design by Design by Committee
Typeset in 12/18.5 Garamond Premier Pro by J&M Typesetting
Proudly printed in Australia by Griffin Press

The paper this book is printed on is certified against the Forest Stewardship Council®
Standards. Griffin Press holds FSC chain of custody certification SGS-COC-005088. FSC
promotes environmentally responsible, socially beneficial and economically viable management of the world's forests.

BEST
AUSTRALIAN
COMEDY
WRITING

EDITED BY LUKE RYAN

Contents

Introduction

Comedians and jazz musicians are more comforting to me than preachers or politicians or philosophers or poets or painters or novelists. Historians in the future, in my opinion, will congratulate us on very little other than our clowning and our jazz.

– Kurt Vonnegut

When Affirm Press asked me to compile an anthology on Australia's finest jazz writing, I could hardly contain my excitement. Finally, a chance to riff with like-minded tromboners and rhapsodise about the intrinsic bebop of the humble bassoon. When they suggested that I had misinterpreted the tenor of their Vonnegut-wrapped request (those ingrates), I instead cast my mind back to an experience at the Edinburgh Fringe Festival a few years ago.

1

The Edinburgh Fringe is basically comedy's version of Mecca, a relentless four-week orgy of artistic heartbreak, penury and high-grade alcoholism that every comedian really needs to experience at least once in their lives. At about four one morning, I was chatting with a British guy named Jeremy, dissecting the success of the UK's comedy scene over a graveyard of empty pints. At one point Jeremy stopped and said, 'You know what Australia's problem is? It doesn't take comedy seriously enough.' This sentiment so offended my sensibilities that I stood up, swept my hand in outrage, and accidentally broke four pint glasses.

Jeremy is right, of course, though I wouldn't let the country down by admitting it at the time. While Australia has produced comedy for a long time, we've never quite been able to bring ourselves to give it the respect it deserves. Entertainment, yes. Art, no.

This feels especially true when it comes to the written word. Australia hasn't developed the grand tradition of humour writing and literary satire that fills the American and English canons, from Mark Twain and Kurt Vonnegut to PG Wodehouse, authors who paved the way for modern masters such as David Sedaris, Simon Rich, Nora Ephron and Terry Pratchett. While we're hardly devoid of exceptional comedic voices in this country, we still seem to find it difficult to believe that funny writing might have literary merit. It all smacks too much of easy enjoyment, and Literature, as we usually conceive it, is a swirl of miserabilism and suffering tied together with historical curios and the occasional exotic location. Jokes have about as much place in your typical high-minded novel as a piercing insight into the human condition does on an episode of *Family Feud*.

Aren't we short-changing comedy here? Underestimating its technical difficulty and capacity to illuminate the human condition? Because comedy writing is a tough art. It requires concision, precision and an intuitive sense of how the reader is going to formulate your sentences in their mind. It needs a poet's grasp of language, an encyclopaedic knowledge of culture, high and low, and a vast array of euphemisms for embarrassing bodily functions. More than anything, it takes a sharpened instinct for what people will actually find funny. You can learn the rules that govern joke writing, but they won't help unless you understand what the joke actually is.

Comedy is also a broad and sometimes profound church. Whatever the event, comedy has an answer. It can be a vehicle for confession and redemption, for political manifestos and biting satire, for well-crafted idiocy and out-and-out lunacy. You'll find examples of them all inside these pages.

The twenty-four pieces of comedic writing that you're about to discover are by turns uplifting, mordant, sad, thought-provoking and just plain stupid. Sometimes they're all of them at the same time. You'll find the best of Australia's books, magazines, online satire and Twitter feeds, as well as a dozen newly commissioned works that represent the latest and greatest in Australian written comedy. Some of the pieces are embarrass-yourself-on-public-transport funny, others will leave you nodding your head in thought, like you finally understood one of the cartoons in the *New Yorker*. There are non-stop gag-fests and slow-burning memoirs, offbeat parodies and surrealist wonderlands. There are some of this country's most revered comic voices and some of the bright young things we'll be laughing at for decades to come. I hope that you'll enjoy exploring them as much as I did bringing them together.

If a decade of watching, performing and writing comedy has taught me anything, it's that throwing the word 'best' in front of the word 'comedy' is like throwing a bright red tablecloth in front of a hormonal bull. Whereas drama attracts gentler criticisms, there's something about comedy we dislike that really fires up the blood. It's not merely bad, it's a personal insult, and everyone who likes it should be taken out the back and shot. If you think I'm overstating things, just try and tell me that you've ever had a civilised conversation with someone who sincerely loved *Two and a Half Men*.

So let me finish by saying that you won't love everything in this book. Some of it you may outright hate. But, hey, even if you do, at least you'll be taking it seriously. Read it and weep, Jeremy.

LAWRENCE LEUNG

Fear and Clothing in North Fitzroy

‘Former Housemate Grace introduced me to her friend. She smiled and looked at Grace with a raised eyebrow that I knew meant: 'Lawrence? As in, *that* Lawrence?'’

It was going to take all my willpower to enter the bookshop. All I needed to do was to buy a present for my mother's birthday. However, in my hand was a novel that I had been reading on the bus. It was my book, but it still looked brand-new because I like to take care of my possessions. With nowhere to stash it, I was going to have to do it: enter the shop and risk looking like a shoplifter. My palms started to sweat.

I've always had this weird phobia of being wrongly accused of a crime. I can't seem to find a specific name for this affliction on Wikipedia or Doctor Google, but if there is one, I'm sure there must be an obscure German word for it. For me, it's a chronic and persistent phobia of looking dodgy.

I realised I was hovering in the doorway, looking ... well, dodgy. So I took a deep breath and began crumpling a few pages of my paperback. The book started to look pre-owned, well-read, slightly abused. *Ugh. This is not going to look good on the bookshelf next to all my pristine book spines.*

'Lawrence?'

Two young women were standing at the shopfront, staring at me.

The one who had spoken was Former Housemate Grace.*

'Oh. Grace. Hello,' I spluttered.

'What are you up to?'

She was looking at the mangled, sweaty paperback in my hands. I felt my face getting hot. How long had they been watching me? I managed to squeeze out a 'Long time no see'.

Former Housemate Grace introduced me to her friend. She smiled and looked at Grace with a raised eyebrow that I knew meant: 'Lawrence? As in, *that* Lawrence?'

I can't remember the rest of the small talk, but I know I entered the shop feeling twice as dodgy as before.

My looking-dodgy-phobia is crippling and absurd. It's that niggling fear that everyone inside a JB Hi-Fi is an undercover security guard, burning me with their eyes. It's the reason I sweat when a police car pulls up next to my car at traffic lights, despite the fact I am doing nothing.

It's got so bad now that I even cross the road whenever there is a lone person on the footpath ahead of me at night. I just don't want them to think I'm following them, or have designs on their wallet. Once I hid behind a tree, waiting for an old lady to disappear from view around the corner. Surely she couldn't be frightened of me if she didn't know I was there. In that moment I realised I am less afraid of being mugged than of people thinking I'm a mugger.

I blame the movies. Every second thriller is about some ordinary Joe who is wrongly accused of killing his wife/sidekick/President and becomes a fugitive. What would you do if you were on the run? Naturally, you'd try to clear your name by finding the real murderer.

---

* Grace is not her real name but rather her general disposition in the share house we used to live in.

Soon you become so driven in your obsessive quest, you end up morphing into the heartless animal they accused you of being, culminating in your brutal slaying of the real killer. It's intense, poignant, but what have you become? At this point in the movie, you have no choice but to dramatically punch a mirror.

It seems the major side effect of wrongly-accused-phobia is that the more you are afraid of being a suspect the more you sound suspicious to everyone else. If you protest innocence, you look more guilty. As the old adage from the playground goes: 'Whoever smelt it, dealt it.' And I'm terrified of looking like I dealt a ripper.

Recently, I explained my phobia to a slightly inebriated neurosurgeon who I met at a party. His name was Marcus and he had the annoying habit of beginning every sentence with a disclaimer:

'I'm not saying there's any formal scientific evidence for hypnosis, but I have friends who swear by it.'

'I'm not speaking for everyone on the planet, but aren't most people afraid of being wrongly accused?'

'I'm not a psychiatrist, but your phobia doesn't sound unusual at all.'

Marcus' phobia was of accidentally paralysing or killing a patient during brain surgery.

'I'm not saying my phobia is more rational than yours, Lawrence, but my phobia has consequences that affect reputations, patients and their families.'

I'm not saying he wasn't a bit of a dick, but despite his arrogance, he was right. My own phobia sounded less hardcore than his.

To regain some footing in the conversation, I needed to demonstrate my fear with a concrete example. So I told him about the incident with Former Housemate Grace.

I had moved into a share house in North Fitzroy. It was one of those old terraces with hip-yet-kitsch antique furniture and housemates who practised Adulthood cosplay. Up until that point I had only ever lived with the two people who had created me and one fellow womb-mate. Living with people I wasn't related to was a completely alien concept, so I didn't want to get off on the wrong foot.

At the time, my only knowledge of share-house living came from *He Died with a Felafel in His Hand* and *Single White Female*, so I was well aware of the things that could leave a bad impression as a housemate: heroin, bongs and getting an identical haircut to Bridget Fonda's. Before helping me load my last box into the car, my older brother sat me down and explained that in any share house, one flatmate will be the odd one out, the person who's one MSG sachet short of a Mi Goreng packet.

'Lawrence,' he said in that patronising way that only an older sibling can pronounce, 'if you don't know who the odd one out is ... it's you.'

I was determined to be the least dodgy one in the house. Perhaps in this new environment my phobia of looking suspicious would, finally, be an advantage. Surely it was a superpower that could give me a heightened sense of whether I appeared unusual, and I could prevent myself from being the odd one out.

Unfortunately, I was the only one in the house with a Y chromosome. My housemates were three brilliant women: an artist, an academic and a fashion designer. They dressed in *Frankie* magazines and floated around pretty antique furniture while the music of vinyl albums from yesteryear filled the air. I was in *Mad Men*, but without the cigarettes and Men.

Maybe they were looking for a Real Man to move into the house, but instead what they got was me. I don't follow sport, I drive automatic transmission and I cry during every Pixar film. Even *Cars*. Determined to appear normal, I did all the apparently manly things required of me. I killed spiders. I tried fixing the washing machine. I rang the washing machine repairman to fix what I had done to it. For a few weeks, I didn't blow my cover. Then, one morning, the storm clouds gathered over me. Literally.

I was looking out the window, daydreaming about being Houdini, when I noticed that the sky had become distinctly morbid – something that I should have taken as an omen. I grabbed the washing basket and started taking my T-shirts down from the clothesline. The final thing left up was my Chewbacca beach towel. As I gave it a tug, it was drawn away like a curtain, revealing a long row of delicate underwear. They were not mine. They stared back at me like silky French sparrows perched daintily on a powerline.

I found myself with an ethical dilemma. I could be a good housemate and carry the foreign washing out of the rain. But my phobia of looking dodgy was telling me: 'You are new to this house. You do not touch someone else's intimate apparel.'

So I took only my clothes in.

Through the window, the clouds were getting darker, threatening the petite pastel panties that clung onto the line like fragile notes on sheet music.

My two anxieties began battling it out, with politeness berating looking-dodgy-phobia. *I should bring them inside. It's the good thing to do, right? I'm helping out a housemate.* The wind picked up, and the lacy lady briefs flapped like tiny flags on the tail of an out-of-control kite.

I grabbed the basket again.

I stood inside the lounge room with a small pile of my housemate's knickers. *Should I just leave them unceremoniously dumped on the couch?* Politeness flared up again; it didn't look right. *Should I fold them? How do females fold these? Is it like cutting a sandwich? I like my sandwiches cut into rectangles. My mum cuts them in triangles. Mum's a female – I should fold them in triangles. It's the polite thing to do.*

But here's the problem. Whenever I take down the washing from the clothesline in the morning, I cannot tell whether the garment is still wet or merely cold. It's weird, and there is probably an obscure German word for this, too, but my skin cannot tell the difference between the sensation of slightly damp and the sensation of coolness. The only way I can fathom the difference between cold (yet dry) and slightly damp is to rub the garment against some sensitive skin. Like my cheek. So I did.

I grabbed a couple of cotton undies in each hand and massaged them against my face.

Then my phobia kicked in. It was like Peter Parker's spider-sense. I got the uncanny feeling that I was ... being watched. Housemate Grace was standing in the doorway carrying shopping bags. She stared at me. I removed my face from her panties. She continued to stare. I slowly placed them back onto the pile. She avoided eye contact as she continued past me and into her bedroom. As the door closed behind her, I blurted out, 'I was just checking if they were still wet!'

In the years since, I have thought about this incident more than I should. I'm not saying I lose sleep over it or get horrifying flashbacks whenever I see underwear ads on a billboard. It's just my strongest reminder of the curious fear I have of looking like I've done something wrong when really I'm innocent.

'I don't live there anymore,' I told Marcus the neurosurgeon.

He put down his glass with a smug *clink*.

'Wetness is a perceptual illusion,' he began. 'If you put on a rubber glove and stick your finger into a glass of water, your brain will tell you your finger is wet, even though you know it is dry. Your skin receptors can sense temperature, pressure, even slipperiness, but they can't actually sense whether things are wet.'

'No way.'

'Yes way. Your brain is lying to you. If you close your eyes and I hold a cold spoon to your cheek, you could swear your face was wet. It's completely normal not being able to tell wet from cold.'

This was great news. 'So if I explain this to her – as the reason why I was rubbing her underwear on my face – she'll understand, right?'

I was practically begging him to say that science can prove my innocence. He opened his palms to the heavens, Woody Allen-style. 'I'm not saying I could speak for her, as I don't know her, but it's the truth.'

They say a process of gradual desensitisation can cure a phobia. This involves gradually increasing exposure to the very thing that elicits the fear. If you are scared of spiders, they get you to stare at the word 'SPIDER'. Then draw a picture of a spider. Then touch a photo of a spider. Then hold a live tarantula while wearing a Spiderman costume.

That night I composed about eleven drafts of an email to Former Housemate Grace. I explained the scene from my point of view; how the skin mistakes pressure and temperature for the sensation of dampness; how I did nothing wrong.

I never clicked 'SEND' on the email. My phobia told me that sending an email out of the blue, years after the incident, would result in the polar opposite of what the email was intended for.

My phobia of looking dodgy is telling me to stop writing any more of this.

LALLY KATZ

Flowers

❛Maria had made quite a point of telling me that I must not shame her by the corpse of Jovanka. 'You should to dress in all black, with the hair up and the earring. Do not walk like crazy person two hour to my house wearing the bad shoe and rubbish.'❜

I was in Sydney for work, and I was meant to be going to Brisbane with my boyfriend to watch a talk he was doing about his book the next day. We hadn't seen much of each other for a while because of work travel. I was really excited about going with him. And more than that, I was really excited that he wanted me to go. It was slightly out of character for him to want company. I felt like maybe this would begin a new chapter in our relationship.

My mobile phone rang. 'Lally,' whispered the Hungarian-accented voice on the other end. It was Maria, my 86-year-old former neighbour.

'Maria, are you okay?' Maria and I talked on the phone most days. And most days it was about an emergency. Such as she'd run out of pasta dura bread, or her back was sore, or a letter had arrived in the post. I called her with emergencies too. Usually romantic ones.

'Jovanka is ... died. Her daughter call and tell me. She is died.'

'Maria, no. Not Jovanka.' Jovanka was Maria's Serbian frenemy. Jovanka was also one of the most popular characters I'd ever written. She featured in my play about Maria, *Neighbourhood Watch*.

'She was never sick. I am more sick than her. Why should she to died? Is not fair. Maria is sick too!'

'She always looked pretty sick, Maria.' Maria has raged against Jovanka since I met her. Suspecting her of laughing at her behind her back, tricking her and not coming to visit her. But from the outside, it always looked to me like Jovanka really wanted to be Maria's friend.

'I don't ring her. Because she should to ring me. I never ring the Jovanka before she has died. I am very sad.'

'Maria, the Jovanka know you love her.'

'She was big bastard to me.'

'I'm so sorry, Maria.'

'Lally, the Jovanka family call me. They wanting me to come sit and watch the Jovanka dead body with them. I like to go. I like to show everyone that Maria can do it. Maria go very glamour and she make the peace. No matter how cruelty the person.'

'I think you should go, Maria.'

'But, Lally, I need you come with me. Please. I never ask you for nothing else. Just come sit by the corpse of Jovanka with me tomorrow.'

'Maria, I think the family will think that's strange.'

'They know you. They love you because the Jovanka all the time love you. Please.'

A few things ran through my head. One, I was meant to be going to Brisbane with my boyfriend – I wanted to go to Brisbane with my boyfriend. I felt so sure that it was going to be the thing that made our relationship. Two, I felt it would be awkward if I went and sat by the corpse of Jovanka. I had met her husband, but no one else in the family. Three, I am a writer and I am hungry for experiences. And one of my favourite characters had died. My very favourite character was going to sit by her corpse. I wanted to be there too. I would never forgive myself if I missed this story.

I called my boyfriend. 'I'm coming back to Melbourne tonight.'

'Why don't you just fly from Sydney and meet me in Brisbane tomorrow?' he asked.

'Jovanka's died. Maria wants me to come and sit by her corpse.'

'You should do that.'

'I'm sorry.'

'Don't be sorry. You have to go with Maria.'

We hung up. I was sad. Decisions always feel so high-stakes, like you're always choosing between one possible life and another.

Back in Melbourne the next day, I walked the two-hour walk to Maria's house, buying pasta dura bread on the way. Maria had made quite a point of telling me that I must not shame her by the corpse of Jovanka. 'You should to dress in all black, with the hair up and the earring. Do not walk like crazy person two hour to my house wearing the bad shoe and rubbish.' I'd decided to risk walking, but carried high heels and a heavy dry-cleaning bag of black grieving clothes.

I rang Maria's bell. She opened the door wearing an old jumper, and her hair was very frizzy. This was certainly not how I'd expected Maria to dress for sitting by Jovanka's corpse.

'I just have to change,' I told her.

'Ja.' She nodded and walked over to the stove where she was cooking soup.

'Don't you have to change?' I asked her.

'No. Maria don't change. Don't rush. Have the soup first.'

'But you said we have to be there five o'clock, no later.'

Maria looked at me. 'We are not going.'

'We're not going?'

'No, why should we to go and sit by the corpse of the Jovanka with the family? You who don't know the family – no I don't like that. Her daughter very nice call and say she pick me up, take me, but I no going. Rest of the Serbs will push me down. No, we are not going. Instead we go to florist and get one very beautiful wreath, Serbian colour, that we take on the funeral tomorrow morning.'

'But you said we were going to see Jovanka today. That's why I brought these clothes over –'

'Ja, you wear them to funeral tomorrow.'

I realised that I was here for nothing. I'd cancelled going to Brisbane, and now we weren't even going to sit by Jovanka's body. 'Well, I have to tell you, Maria, I'm very angry. Because you're always telling me that I change the plan, but I don't change the plan, you change the plan! You said we were going to see Jovanka's dead body, and now you change the plan!'

'Ja, because now I got better plan!'

'Well, I was meant to be going to Brisbane with the boyfriend and I change so I can come with you to sit with the Jovanka's body.'

'You never tell me that! Why you tell me that now? Why you come here and then say I should to be there instead of here. You hurt me very much. The Jovanka has died and you is hurting me.'

There was no winning this. I'd made my choice. And Maria was right. Her best frenemy had died. 'I'm sorry, Maria. I'm just sad because I wanted to see the Jovanka.'

Maria brightened. 'Don't be sad for that! You will see the Jovanka! Tomorrow morning when we go to funeral is open casket!'

After eating soup, Maria got dressed and we caught a taxi to the florist she liked. As we got out of the taxi, I realised something. 'Maria, this florist, this is near where Jovanka lived, isn't it?'

'Ja. You were there. Very close lived the Jovanka.'

Maria and I looked for the right flowers. Maria kept asking the short-haired, tattooed florist questions. 'Tell me, how much is these?'

'They're $65. The same as when you asked two minutes ago.' The florist didn't like Maria. She was very busy wrapping pre-orders of flowers. It seemed like a big day for them.

Finally we picked out white roses and took them up to be wrapped in the colours of the Serbian flag. At the counter, Maria muttered, 'But bastard, what is the Serbian flag? I forget.'

'I'll check on my phone,' I offered.

'You can do?'

'Of course.' I googled the Serbian flag. It came up on my phone with three stripes: top red, middle blue and bottom white. 'Here it is, Maria.' I showed her the phone.

'No, Russian. That is the Russia flag.'

'Serbian.'

'Russian.'

I decided the only way to solve this was to search for the Russian flag. It came up the opposite to the Serbian flag: top stripe white, middle stripe blue and bottom stripe red. I showed it to Maria.

'Ja, Russian,' she said.

I brought up the Serbian flag again. 'You see the difference, Maria?'

'Ja, Russian,' she said.

I was beginning to get very angry.

'No, Maria! This is the Serbian flag! The other flag is Russian!'

'Why you all the time so stupid? You tell me you can find Serbian flag but all you find is the Russia!'

'You're the one who's being stupid, not me. This is the Serbian flag.'

'Maria know the Serbian flag, I was married to one Serb. Lally don't know nothing.'

Just then, we were interrupted by a soft voice. A tall woman, probably in her forties, was speaking gently to Maria in Serbian. She was dressed in black, and her eyes were very sad. She was the spitting image of Jovanka.

Maria spoke to her in Serbian for another moment, and then turned to me and said, 'You know who is this?'

'Are you Jovanka's daughter?' I asked her.

She nodded, tears in her eyes.

'I'm so sorry about your mother.'

'She's at peace now.' Part of me, looking at Jovanka's grieving daughter, thought, *Here she is. Here's the story I didn't go to Brisbane for.* And the other part of me thought, *Here she is. She's real and she's so sad. I'm glad I didn't sit with her at her mother's body.*

I asked her, 'Do you know what the colours of the Serbian flag are?'

'Yes. Red, then blue, then white.'

'I told you,' said Maria.

'You did not tell me –' I hissed before reining myself back in.

Jovanka's daughter picked up two wreaths she had ordered for her mother's funeral the next day.

'I am sick too,' Maria told her. 'More sick than the mummy.'

The daughter looked worried, and told Maria to only come to the funeral if she was well enough. She smiled at us, thanked us for getting her mother flowers and left.

Maria watched her leaving and said, 'Very fat. She has grown. Like the mother.'

Maria paid for the flowers. We decided to get another taxi instead of the tram. After all, we had a big night ahead of us, preparing for the funeral.

Two months later, my boyfriend and I would break up.

Originally appeared in The Monthly, *June 2014*

ANDREW DENTON

Welcome to HED 2015

❛Let me share with you just a few of the milestones that have made HED the pre-eminent place for people actively engaged in 'talking about doing things' to gather.❜

Welcome, fellow Earthians, to HED talks 2015, tonight coming to you from Sydney, Australia.

On this very day, twenty years ago, the first HED talks were given in a geodesic yurt in Costa Rica, the brainchild of Feldenkrais guru Françoise Musk and ethical burrito franchise billionaire Tip Wilson.

Their dream: to create a space where people could come together and solve all the world's problems by talking about them. A lot. With pictures. And, ideally, music.

The programme for that first conference was only four talks, but each one set a new standard for public discourse. Let me remind you of those first, seminal, presentations:

Skylar Pascaarl's moving *What I've Learned from My Profoundly Deaf, Vegetarian and Angry Neighbour.*

Dr Luce Schwitter's revolutionary *Why Breathing Matters.*

The thought-provoking *Re-engineering Zebras to Fight Measles*, presented by the late Professor Zlatco Zemanek, interpretative geneticist.

And, of course, Margaret Fynne's game-changing visual presentation, *How Just Thinking About Poor People Can Make This Graph Different Over Time*. There wasn't a dry eye in the yurt after that one, I can tell you.

Four amazing talks that are as relevant today as they were then.

In the past twenty years, HED talks have taken place in more than fifty countries and, on one occasion in 1999, in 140 hot air balloons roped together above the deserts of Saharan Africa as a show of support for the Tuareg people of Mali.

The three letters that make up the word HED – H for Hype, E for Exaggeration and D for Drama – have proven to be prophetic as, each year, remarkable thinkers have come forward to help us reimagine our universe.

Let me share with you just a few of the milestones that have made HED the pre-eminent place for people actively engaged in 'talking about doing things' to gather.

In 1996, HED Sarajevo saw Jahan El Murad invited to address the United Nations after his presentation, *How a Single Rubber Ball Can End the Conflict in Gaza and Restore Balance in the Middle East*, electrified the conference.

In 1998, at HED Tuvalu, the future was unveiled in front of our very eyes when Pradeep Mandesh of the Bangalore Institute of Technology demonstrated a robot that could exactly replicate most of the dance moves from Pat Benatar's 'Love Is a Battlefield' video.

In 2001, HED Poughkeepsie saw Turkish electric bouzouki virtuoso Istvan Ornek's translation of the Bhagavad Gita into music prompt Peter Gabriel to declare, 'Those were six of the most entrancing hours I have ever spent in my life.'

In 2007, at HED Mogadishu, Lyn Portillo's address, *I Am a Boy Trapped in the Body of a Girl and I Am Dating Myself*, became the first HED talk to get more than 1 million hits on YouTube.

And Thabo Nkwele's provocative 2011 HED Tenerife keynote, *Is Joseph Kony Hiding in the Cloud?*, continues to stir debate around the globe.

But HED is about more than just talking. In 2004, the first HED Scholarships were announced, rewarding 'Ideas That Sound Great When You First Hear Them'.

Winners that year included Patsy Squelch, who showed us how to crowdsource our own breakfast, and Diwash Biryani who demonstrated that, over time, badgers could be trained to harmonise using simple melodies.

Of course, HED has its critics. But for those who doubt that it is a powerful agent for change, just one example: in 1997, Jed Campbell presented a compelling argument that small acts of sacrifice in the first world could completely eliminate poverty in the third world. Campbell's plan, outlined in this famous graph designed by Ziggy Woltare from the KAPOW! Kollective, was hailed as a breakthrough in simplifying the complexities of world aid.

Today, eighteen years later, as a direct result of Campbell's HED talk, I am proud to tell you that more than five million African households now have a copy of this graph up on their walls. Many in colour. Yes, you may well clap.

I am also pleased to tell you that the HED Travelling Fellows Programme – established in 2008 – continues to make a difference. After the initial success of Sharon Stone's fact-finding mission to the Middle East, we have since sent Dennis Rodman to North Korea to help normalise relations with that county's troubled regime, and, most recently, One Direction to the Taliban heartland of Waziristan in northern Pakistan as 'Hopefulness Ambassadors'. That was a few weeks ago. We still haven't heard anything, which we are taking as a positive sign.

Tonight, Musk and Wilson's self-styled 'Mochaccino Revolution' continues and, as always, it features some of the innovations for which HED has become famous:

For people who are not quite as important as you, there are nearby 'simulcast' lounges where they can share in the HED experience on large screens.

For those here tonight who may become overwhelmed by the intensity of the ideas, the Steve Jobs Worship Room – where you can sit quietly and just think about Steve – is back.

The ever-popular firewalking pit, as always generously sponsored by KFC, will also be open. Though, once again, a reminder to parents: please don't leave kids unattended, no matter how well their chakras are aligned.

And, of course, beginning tonight, there is our unrivalled programme of speakers, headlined this year by Freelance Happiness Consultant Debbi Nasht with her game-changing talk, *How I Used Facebook, Twitter, Instagram and Tumblr to Tell the World I Need to Be Alone.*

Immediately after Debbi, over on the Panasonic Gaia Stage, HED is honoured this year to hear from the father of the internet, Tim Berners-Lee, with his talk, *Did I Mention That I Invented the Internet?*

Then at midnight we will be crossing live via satellite to the Middle East, where The Kinetic Philosopher himself, Dr Flint Edema, will be giving a remarkable demonstration of the power of stories to change the world. From an elevated platform in southern Turkey, Flint will be broadcasting humorous anecdotes through one thousand-kilowatt speakers across the Syrian border and directly into some of the region's outlying ISIS camps.

As you watch Flint subtly change our world, I urge you to keep in mind the deepest truth about HED: whether you are motivated to do something or not, what's most important is that you can say, 'I was there.' Especially to people who were not.

Before I introduce Debbi, it seems appropriate that I go back to that first HED conference twenty years ago and ask you to join me in repeating the call and response affirmation that Wilson and Musk used to announce the arrival of a new way of thinking to the world.

I want to hear a loud 'YES!' to each of these questions: Are you aware? Are you centred? Are you important?

Then say it after me. 'I *am* self-aware. I *am* self-centred. I *am* self-important.'

Give yourself a round of applause then hug the person next to you.

Now kiss them lightly on the lips.

Now stroke their inner thigh.

Welcome to HED 2015.

ZOË NORTON LODGE

Almost Sincerely

‘While my friends learned that men can be cruel, I learned that sometimes when you go into a shop, people feel sorry for you and give you stuff for free. My friends were in Cancun, and I was in a Kafka story.’

How Come Why for Did You Call My Friend Denise a Bitch

Mamma was one strict lady when I was growing up. Playtime at the park directly next to our house was limited to short spurts in high daylight and supervised by Mamma, who could see me always through all the windows along the east wing of our family home. It didn't matter whether she was knitting a scarf, making a Nescafé or watching *Wheel of Fortune*. Whatever she was doing, she was also watching me in the park. Trees were not for climbing, and legs were not for running. That's how I grew up to be in a rare subset of ethnically Mediterranean people with the pallor of jellyfish. Should a sleepover be on the cards, Mamma always required a detailed itinerary of any goings-on and their proximity to major roads and rapists, and I was walked to school until long after I developed the ability to menstruate.

If horror films have taught us anything, it's those sleepy little suburbs where nothing much ever happens, where the doors are always unlocked and the children unwatched, it's those types of places, the world's Annandales, where the terrible thing will definitely happen. Now, Mamma didn't really like horror movies. She was more of a *Judge*

31

Judy type of woman. But lessons are everywhere, and *Judge Judy* taught a very similar syllabus on the perils of living in a boring residential postcode.

And then one day, after twelve steely years of watching and waiting, the moment came that Mamma had been preparing for all my life.

I was playing in the park with my long-term collaborators Sally and Dwayne. We'd been tight since preschool, and the main base for our operations was the park between our houses. There were further (temporary) members of our council, but if we three were there then quorum was met and we could discuss business – which usually focused on matters such as which of the dogs that always fought in the park would die first; whose parents were *real* alcoholics and which were fair-weather benders; who currently had cake in their house; and which teachers were probably having sex with each other and which others should be fired for being perverts.

One autumn Year 6 day, we were sitting up the top of the slippery dip discussing whose dad was the most drunkest the most often. It was definitely a close race, we all agreed, but nonetheless, each passionately advocated our personal dad to be the most loaded the most regularly. I was quietly prosecuting the case for my own dad – pointing to the sneakiness of his drinking many half-bottles of chardonnay as evidence in favour of his superiority over Sally and Dwayne's dad – when I heard someone calling from the bottom of the slide.

'Oi!'

It was an older girl. She had straight red hair that had been pulled over and over through an iron, possibly a clothes iron, because it was baked and cauterised at the tips. From the very middle of her forehead, two tiny plaits sprung out of her hairline and arced down her face, weighted at the bottom with pink baubles. She had brutal pencil lines where her eyebrows might have been and she had undone all the bottom buttons of her white school blouse and tied it in a knot, exposing an infected yin-yang bellybutton ring.

She was standing just in front of another girl, whose school kilt was high and tight and framed by a jumper that was tied around her waist. She wore a pink plastic crucifix that nestled into her significant cleavage, and her dyed black hair was tied so tightly into a bun as to give her the impression of having had too much work done. Everything about them was remote and discomforting. Whatever these things were, they weren't from Annandale.

'I said, oi! Girl!'

'What?' I said.

She looked up at me at the top of the slippery dip.

'Tell me how come why for did you call my friend Denise a bitch?'

'Who's *Denise*?' I said, with an inflection that implied that I did not think Denise was a nice name, even though I secretly did, and also had the effect of seeming like I hadn't even noticed her friend, even though I definitely had.

'Get down here,' she said.

And me, with the confidence of someone who has always lived in Annandale, who knows that nothing bad ever happens in the park, slid down and stood in front of the teenage miscreants, arms folded.

'I didn't even say *anything*,' I said.

The girl's eyes widened. The other girl, who I presumed was Denise, didn't look at me. She just picked the day's filth out of her long, pink nails.

'How come why for are you now calling my friend Denise a liar?'

'*What?*' I said, and the girl raised her arm. She raised her arm, dripping with glowing, glittery plastic bracelets, she pulled it back and then, before I had any idea what was happening, slapped me hard across the face, digging her acrylic nails into my cheek and dragging them across in her follow-through.

I looked at her. Completely stunned. I never knew that there could be any negative consequences for just telling the truth. But there I was. All slapped.

I was about to stammer out something. I had no idea what it was going to be, when the other girl, Maybe-Denise, ran at me gridiron-style, her massive boobs swinging wildly, like angry pendulums, as she closed in and pushed me backwards into the dirt.

And that was the moment.

All the autumn leaves on the ground began to rustle, and all the little blades of grass in the park stiffened beneath them. The clouds in the sky thickened as they drew closer together then joined, and everything became dull.

Then a huge gust of wind blew through the park. It blew all the way through the park to my house, and it blew the front door of my house wide open.

And there was Mamma, standing in the doorway of our house, and she was bright. Everything else was grey, but Mamma was bright. She was bright because she was backlit by every scented candle in Annandale, flaming behind her down the hallway of our house. And she stood still, as the wind swirled the little lit wicks of the candles behind her and the trees around the house and all the autumn leaves on the ground in the park and the last of the leaves that were still in the trees all swirled in the wind, but Mamma stood still, her eyes locked on us, on the mess in the park that we were.

And as we watched her, she slowly parted her arms, dripping in the black silk of her *Judge Judy*-watching kimono, and she splayed out all of her ten ringed fingers. She looked those two girls dead in the eyes as she bent her knees and sprung off the front porch and into the air.

Mamma was in the air, and she was flying. She flew over our gate and across the road and into the park, darting through the trees, twisting and turning, her black kimono flying out behind her, her black hair flying out behind her and her espadrilles never even almost touching the pavement.

And she flew way above us. Way above me on the ground and above Maybe-Denise and the other one and even above Sally and Dwayne at the top of the slippery slide.

And she hovered above us, spinning, around us all, in a slow circle. She spun above her prey, above her treasured ward and above the spectators. She could have grabbed them there and then, her prey, but that was no fun, Mamma wanted to see some bitches run.

Maybe-Denise got up and started to run. And then the other one did too. They started to run through the park, and just as they were about to disappear out of sight, Mamma began to fly, faster than before, her arms and legs stretched out as she glided through the air breaking every speed limit of every transport that ever was. She was bat and she was bullet streaming through the air and then out of the park and down the hill and out of our sight.

Sally and Dwayne and I looked at each other.

'Your mum is really mad,' said Dwayne.

'Yeah,' I said, solemnly.

'And I'll tell you something, I'll never be able to play in the park again.'

'Ever,' added Sally.

A few minutes later we saw the two girls walking back into the park, trying desperately not to look frightened. Mamma was behind them, marching them forward, a hand pressed into each of their backs, and then she sat them both down on a park bench.

'You girls are in deep shit,' she said, leaning against a tree.

'Sally, go to your house and call the cops.'

'What?' said Maybe-Denise.

'Don't even call the cops!' said the other one.

'You, don't talk,' said Mamma. 'You okay?' she asked me.

'Yeah, I'm fine.'

'Don't wash your face, don't wash anything until the cops come and take a photo of your injuries.'

'She wasn't *injured,*' said Maybe-Denise.

'I. Said. Don't. Talk. I've missed the second case of *Judge Judy* now, and I'm not in the mood to hear your voice,' said Mamma, still leaning against the tree and not looking at Maybe-Denise.

The police came and took the girls away. They were pleading and crying, and Mamma watched on, glistening with hero-sweat and smoking a Pall Mall Mild, with a distinct absence of mercy in her eyes.

After that I really thought I would never be able to play in the park again. That wasn't entirely true, but Mamma made Dad go have his after-work half-bottles of chardonnay in the park with Sally and Dwayne's dad every day after that.

This was pretty good, because our dads were not as good at knowing what we were and weren't supposed to be doing. Also, it made it much easier for us to decide who was the most drunkest every day.

The Persistence of Memory

One chilly winter morning, I woke up from the slumber of a twenty-year-old who has the world at her feet, but for some reason works at a discount menswear store. I pondered, unfondly, on the day that stretched out before me of selling cheaply made suits to men who probably shouldn't be proposing to their girlfriends.

After a little tiff with my sleepy, stubborn body, I managed to coax it out of bed. Just before I got to the kitchen to fix a breakfast of whatever the opposite of champions are, I caught a glimpse of myself in the mirror in the hallway.

How interesting, I thought, as I gazed upon my face. *The right side of my face looks normal, and the left side of my face looks like a basset hound.* I touched it, expecting it to be extremely tender, but it was rather more like poking a raw steak. A cold, dead steak.

I did a quick search of my brain to ascertain where this fit in the scheme of things my face should look like. I had on occasion awoken to realise that I had fallen asleep on a corduroy cushion, and then discovered, in the looking glass, a face blotted with deep and squiggly red lines. This was somewhat like that – if, following that event, someone had shot me in the left side of my face with a tranquiliser dart.

I walked to the kitchen and poured myself a bowl of cornflakes. I sat down to eat them, and as I pushed a silvery spoon, quivering with milk and flakes, into my mouth, I thought: *How interesting*. Usually when I perform this rudimentary task, the cornflakes manage to remain in my mouth before embarking on a mysterious journey through my insides. They don't dribble slowly out onto the dining-room table making a very sad clumpy puddle of white and orange gunk. But my mouth couldn't

37

close. Try as I might, the left side of my mouth just gaped slowly in and out, never fully opening or closing, like a fish out of water.

Georgia, who was fourteen at the time and had no understanding of what it meant to toil at a discount menswear store, came into the room.

'Zoë ...' she said as she gazed upon me and the mess I was still in the process of making on the floor. *That's unusual*, I thought as I watched her eyes widen in horror. *My sister doesn't usually look at me like I'm dying.*

'Zoë. Your face is broken.'

In comes Mamma. *Oh, Mamma*, I thought. *She will bring a needed air of calmness and perhaps a fitting explanation for the circumstances. Mamma knows what's what.*

That's weird, I thought, as Mamma took a step back from me, gasped, and burst into tears. *Mamma doesn't usually behave like she's just watched ten puppies get stabbed when she comes to join me in a bowl of morning cornflakes.* She ran out of the room and dialled the doctor. Then she marched me, still in my pyjamas, down the street to our local GP. I sat in the waiting room among a bunch of coughing old ladies and elderly men in grey woollen waistcoats who farted and read the various useless inserts from the paper that had been discarded by previous patients.

Occasionally one or another would look up at me, and their glances would linger on my face. *That's odd*, I thought. Usually it is I gazing upon these aged citizens of the community with a mixture of pity and dread, and it seems that the tables have turned.

Then my turn came. The doctor came out.

'Zoë?' she said, looking at me and then immediately down at her clipboard. 'Right this way.'

'It seems half of my face is broken,' I told the doctor, as I sat down in the little white room, adorned with crayon pictures and photos of toddlers. She pulled out a packet of baby wipes and considered my face with a mild mixture of sorrow and disgust, like a pigeon that had been run over by a bicycle. Not quite dead, but certainly not quite right.

'I think you have Bell's palsy.'

'What's that?'

'No one really knows.'

'Is there anything I can do?'

'Take steroids.'

'What will they do?'

'Look, probably nothing, but they will make you put on quite a lot of weight.'

'In that sense, those steroids are a bit like fifty Big Macs.'

'I suppose.'

'Is there anything else I should know?'

'You'll need to buy an eye patch.'

'Why?'

'Because your left eye will weep a constant stream of tears until it goes away.'

'When will it go away?'

'Who can say. Could be a month, could be seven years.'

I left the doctor's surgery with a prescription for steroids and another for heavy painkillers, which I definitely didn't need, but I dutifully took, because when science tells me I am allowed drugs, I am at her mercy. At the chemist I also bought my eye patch, which I found out soon after would be my best friend – if one's best friend made one look like a sad pirate.

As a twenty-year-old, I had been, until that very morning, skipping merrily down the same sexy path of experimentation as my friends. Then two roads diverged in a yellow wood. While my friends learned that men can be cruel, I learned that sometimes when you go into a shop, people feel sorry for you and give you stuff for free. My friends were in Cancun, and I was in a Kafka story.

I quickly learned the following about Bell's palsy: It makes half your face look like Salvador Dalí's melting clocks. Doctors really don't know anything about it, but they'll chemically fatten you while you have it because there's a character-building exercise somewhere in the Hippocratic Oath. Tissues are your constant bedfellow due to the Bell's palsy mouth maxim: what goes in, must dribble slowly out.

I tried my best to maintain a normal, *Sex and the City*-inspired social life. On Friday night I'd go out for drinks with my girlfriends. Camilla would tell us how the Chilean bartender downstairs just asked for her number, and I'd tell the gang about Mamma crying while watching me try to drink through a straw.

Of all the people in my life, myself included, Mamma was the most upset by my new face. She even took it upon herself to do some internet research. She had discovered a PDF created by a university in Europe with some helpful advice on how to rehabilitate people with Bell's palsy. It included things like forcing them to chew with the affected side of their mouth, trying to whistle and, of course, trying to drink through a straw. If I had bothered to look it up myself, I'm reasonably confident that I would have discovered that the PDF had in fact been created by the mean older brother of someone with Bell's palsy, for all those tasks were in equal measure demeaning and impossible.

Formerly, at the discount menswear store, I had struggled to move the acres of polyester T-shirts emblazoned with wilfully awful slogans like 'One Tequila, Two Tequila, Three Tequila, Floor', but my new face, which was essentially half a wheel of brie that had been left in the sun and dressed up as a pirate, seemed to evoke a level of pity which induced people to give us money. My canny manager recognised my newfound salesmanship and paraded me around the store like a curious street beggar. She even took me off probation, which meant upgrading my uniform from a polo shirt that said 'Trish' on the pocket to one that said 'Zoë' on the pocket.

My new shirt filled me with pride, and philosophy. I began to become surprisingly self-reflective and ponderous for a sexually excitable twenty-year-old girl.

So, Bell's palsy. It was going to be my thing. It wasn't great, but it could have been worse. I could have been one of those people with an annoying affectation, like always carrying around a ukelele. It probably didn't bode well for my already fruitless attempts to acquire a mate through the tried and tested method of never making eye contact with a man. Cheerfully, things were so barren in that department that this turn of events surely couldn't make things worse. *Perhaps I could even garner a sympathy vote from a biology student*, I thought, hopefully.

I even briefly attempted a gym regimen. Each workout would leave a deep and lasting purple legacy all over my face for at least two hours. Also, each session seemed to bring my breasts one inch closer to my knees, and I already had enough problems in the arena of sagging, so I swapped it for drinking myself into a blissful oblivion.

The days and the months passed, and leaves turned from green to brown to rot, just like the left side of my face, and I grew fatter in dribbling self-acceptance. My friends got used to my expanding form and constantly having to pass me napkins to wipe away the litres of Long Island iced tea dribbling down my shirt. I even managed on one occasion to lure a drunk man, who probably had a thing for pirates, back to my spider web.

And one day, in this state of inner peace, I walked into a Gloria Jean's to buy a coffee.

'NOOOOOOOOOOOOOOOO!!!' A man screamed as I approached the counter.

I was used to pity, but never before had my face provoked a response of unbridled terror in a fully-grown adult. And I shot him the most severe dirty look I was capable of.

I went to leave, and then time froze. I couldn't move. My feet were melding into the floor. Either I was having a night terror or Bell's palsy had migrated to my feet.

I did an inventory of my surroundings. The lights were off. There were no pastries in the darkened counter. I looked back to the entrance and I could see my own footprints. Was I going mad?

I started to feel sick. Like my lungs were filling with chemicals. Which they definitely were.

'What have you done?!' screamed the screaming man with the singular devastation of someone who had, mere moments before, finished several days' work varnishing the floor of a brand-new Gloria Jean's, and now watched helplessly as someone walked in and completely ruined it in an instant.

I looked at him he looked at me. I started to try to run, but very slowly like the sticky Pompeii victim I had become, and gradually progressed away from the screaming man who save from a fist shaking in the air, dared not move, lest he make things worse.

I got outside and tried to walk away, casually, although my sticky footprints leading directly back to the scene of the crime made travelling incognito a challenge. So I called Mamma, who drove over and picked me up a short and sticky distance away from the incident.

We were stopped in the car at a set of lights. Mamma looked at me and started crying. *Great. This is just what I need for my inner peace.*

'Your mouth!' she said.

'I know.'

'No. It looks a little bit more normal!'

I looked in the passenger mirror. It wasn't exactly a *TV Week* smile, but there might have been some movement at the station. I looked at Mamma again.

'You think it's better?'

She considered me for a moment and then started crying again.

'I'm so sorry. I made a mistake. It's still the same.'

'Well … Damn,' I said.

I wound down the window and put my face to the wind and I just let it flap about however it wanted to.

From Almost Sincerely *by Zoë Norton Lodge*
(Giramondo Publishing 2015)

PATRICK LENTON

King of the World

❝As the years ground on, I began to realise the truth of the complex checks and balances required in the political stratosphere. There's always something to consider – finances, zombies, the plotting of my opposition leader, One-Armed Jonathan.❞

I wasn't born a rich man. My father was a part-time oyster shucker who used to hang around restaurants offering to help rich patrons open their seafood. He had thumbnails as hard as roof slate, which he used to jimmy the sharp shells of mussels and scoop out the gelatinous flesh inside. I once saw him use them to slice open the face of a Latino gang leader, a fat thirteen-year-old named Caddy Shack Williams who was trying to expand his territory to the old rotting rowboat we were sleeping in. My dad and I slept in a new boat each night and dined on the molluscs growing underneath, which we cooked gently on a bed of emergency flares.

'God's a shark,' my dad used to say as he pissed into the black water from the back of a yacht. 'Sometimes a man is wading in the shallows, and starts feeling dizzy. When he gets back to the land he discovers a tiger shark has taken his leg, so quick and clean he didn't even feel it. That's called faith. That's what George Michael sang about in that song of his, "Faith".'

My mum was a long-distance swimmer who I only ever saw once, covered in pig fat and swimming in a cage to Tasmania. My dad cried as she passed by, then grabbed me, looked into my eyes and told me, 'Your mum's with God now. I'm going to have to teach you how to strip copper cables from construction sites.'

The point I'm trying to make, my loyal subjects, is that I was poor growing up. Not just economically, but spiritually. I felt I lacked the necessary components for empathy, but whatever, I don't really care about that. So because I was poor, I have to say it never crossed my mind that I would be elected as King of the World. And now here I am, ten years into my reign. It's like a dream but with about 30 per cent less zebra sex.

When I was first elected, I thought I'd have all the sexy power of Thor. I thought that because I was the most important man on the earth, I'd be able to solve world hunger and ride a unicorn to and from the circus. Shit damn, was I naive.

As the years ground on, I began to realise the truth of the complex checks and balances required in the political stratosphere. There's always something to consider – finances, zombies, the plotting of my opposition leader, One-Armed Jonathan. Sure, maybe as a king I could have had a stable of beautiful pink unicorns, but I couldn't because of policy announcements, superannuation, stocks and bonds, gorgonzola, Schwimmer fatigue etc. I don't want to bore you with all my tiresome political jargon, but the point is I'm a much wiser person after my decade of leadership. Fatter, too, but my mentor, Two-Armed Bill, or 'Simply Bill' as he likes to be called, says that wisdom is often manifested by a gland problem.

I'll never forget the day that I discovered I was the new, and first, King of the World. It was unseasonably warm, the sun shining like a self-heating lubricant, the wind stirring golden leaves on the street, puffs of cloud meandering across the sky like old men's heads, and zombies swarming through the cities in a ravening horde of madness and despair. It all seemed to make a terrible kind of sense.

Only a few months earlier, before James Franco bit that ape and started this whole terrible undead shebang, I'd auditioned for a part in hit television show *The Voice*. My dad, who was dying in an old hospice, egged me on to do it.

'What, are you some kind of dickless bird, flapping around in a little bird bath, too scared to sing to a panel of other, larger birds? Like, I dunno, some eagles? Is that it? You a dickless bird?'

I wasn't really offended, as medical nuns had recently castrated him because of his aggressive prostate cancer, so I knew he was probably projecting.

'But I've never sung in my life,' I pointed out. Growing up, if I made any noise over a hoarse whisper, my dad would immediately sink the boat we were sleeping in and make us move cities, convinced the police were onto us.

'You've never sung in your life? Boy, do you think God cares if you've ever sung before? Do you think that would stop God? God would tear Delta Goodrem's rotten face right off her neck, and God can't even breathe on land.'

He'd died not long after that, his face the colour of oysters and safety vests. I went to *The Voice* to audition the next day and sang 'Bad Moon Rising' in honour of my dad, who had been scared of the moon. I wasn't successful, but it was nice to meet Seal, who was a gentleman. After my failure, it seemed only logical that zombies would swamp the world. It was as if my dad's disapproval had come back in the form of a highly contagious undead virus.

When the tide of infection hit, I was drinking away my *Voice* sorrows in my favourite watering hole, an illegal hooch bar named 'Amy Beerhouse'. Beerhouse didn't actually serve beer, just brewed three large bathtubs of eye-watering gin, which patrons scooped out with their hands. You could always tell a regular from Amy

Beerhouse, because of their bleached fingernails and pruned palms, which smelled like juniper.

The proprietor, an ancient Hungarian man named Jononothan, pronounced *Jo-nono-than*, told everyone who visited the bar how he gave Sartre a blowjob in Paris, and how Camus just wanted to be spooned. Jononothan accepted piles of change and pocket lint for his bathtubs of spirits, and sometimes even bartered emotions. I remember seeing a young man who had just become a father trade the sense of panic and responsibility he was feeling for a double handful of gin.

The night the zombie horde limped around the world, it was an uncommonly busy Friday evening at Amy Beerhouse. An indie magazine had recently reviewed the place and mistaken it for a small hip bar. So as well as the regular crowd of murderers and the serially unhappy, there were now middle-aged office workers desperately trying to justify not being asleep, and university students bartering the only two emotions they'd ever experienced, these being wonder and entitlement.

When the zombies initially burst in, people thought it was another raid by the cops. But cops rarely chewed on the fleshy undersides of people's arms, so the patrons eventually fought back. As I wasn't near to an exit and was still sad about the verbal flaying I'd received from Delta Goodrem, I simply sat back and watched.

When the few hundred jaundiced survivors of the zombie apocalypse decided that they needed an elected ruler, I originally didn't think of applying. But then I remembered my dad scraping a layer of mercury from a clam and saying, 'Son, this life is the golden balls. I'm free, don't answer to nobody, and women love an entrepreneur. The only other job I'd ever consider would be the goddamn King of the World.'

I was eight at the time and suffering tonsillitis of the dick, which is actually a thing, not just one of my dad's fake medical diagnoses. I'd said, 'I'd like to be King of the World, Dad.'

He'd looked me up and down and replied, 'Nah. You'll probably just be a ball boy at the tennis.'

My election platform in the first year was simple, my slogan being: 'Vote for me, because my dying dad wanted me to perform on *The Voice* but I failed, but this would also make him posthumously proud of me.' I think this was a pretty emotional time for everybody, because the majority of their loved ones had been eaten and civilisation as we knew it had ended, so people really fell for my sell.

My opponent, One-Armed Jonathan, who at that time had two arms, really misread his audience when he announced his slogan, which was: 'More 1940s era beans for everybody.' It was essentially a platform based entirely on bean distribution.

It's very easy to look back with rose-tinted glasses, but I'm the first to admit I made a lot of mistakes in my first few years in power. I still stand by my decision to have a healthy focus on arts and entertainment. The live performances of episodes of the television show *Friends* that we presented on Friday nights were fun. I agree that my decision to pull the guards away from the southern perimeter so that they could fill the parts of the background characters in the coffee shop in the episode when Chandler proposes to Monica was probably short-sighted, despite it being a really important episode. Yes, I lost the majority of my constituents that night when the zombies overran our unmanned barricades. Yes, One-Armed Jonathan lost his arm. Yes, our nation's innocence was lost. But more importantly than any of that, I lost my complacence.

I heard my opponent, One-Armed Jonathan, giving a speech the other day. He was trying to convince people not to vote for me this year. He said, 'There's only ten of us left now. We're dying in here, you fools, dying. We've run out of beans and our skin is soft and waxy like smegma. Doris has gone blind. My god, I'd rather get eaten than waste away in here. We have to get out, we have to get out, we have to get out.'

If you can read through the false promises and political double-talk, you'll see he's never moved on from his original bean distribution platform. He's also showing his characteristic pessimism – while he thinks there are 90 per cent fewer of us than ten years ago, I like to think there are 100 per cent more. Sue, for example. Sue is a classy lady. Nobody dislikes Sue. Surely this is a good thing? And while I admit that our current lack of beans is troubling, it reminds me of an anecdote from my teenage years.

I was working as a secretary in a law firm, having split from my father a few years earlier. I'd gotten sick of feeling constantly damp and nauseated from the zinc build-up in my guts. I wanted to experience life on the land, to feel money in my hand and to avoid knife fights with transients where the only prize was a seaweed cape. It was barely my second week on the job, and I was staying back late to finish a report my boss wanted the next day. I was also surreptitiously learning how to read analogue time, because I'd never been taught. My dad sidled around the corner of my office, holding the rotting head of a swordfish.

'Son, God came to me last night and in between chewing on the keel of my boat he told me you had to come home. Also, I just shat on the desk of your CEO, and they will blame it on you because we share the same DNA. They have the technology to tell that sort of thing. We have to run, boy.'

We stole some of the thin, sour coffee from the office pots and drank it on a catamaran. My dad had never drunk coffee before, and it made him boisterous and his laugh like a foghorn. He told me we would sail to Vanuatu, Maui and Houston. He also told me about his own father, a celebrity bigamist from the 1940s. But the next morning, his eyes were red and tired, and in a flat voice, he confided that he was scared of the ocean, and also scared of the land, and that people who give up always have a home in the shallows, in the stinking bays and marinas that hug the coast.

I think my point is that while my dad might have been proud of me for being King of the World, he would understand if I gave up and lived under a wharf, eating cockles and riding God's scaly back into the sunset. So on that note, I quit. I officially resign my presidentship. Goodbye. God bless you all.

From A Man Made Entirely of Bats *by Patrick Lenton*
(Spineless Wonders, 2015)

DAVID THORNE

Number Plate People

‘Geoffrey's idea of paying to have the car fixed had consisted of purchasing a bottle of Wynn's Radiator Stop Leak and a new set of wiper blades.’

'We should go to Tasmania,' Geoffrey stated.

He turned his laptop towards me to present a photo of a woman posing on a trail in a rainforest. Geoffrey and I had been friends since working together at a printing firm years before. He was currently employed as a tech specialist for a local sausage manufacturer, and I was in my fourth and final year of design school. It was April 1996.

'Why,' I asked, 'would I want to go to Tasmania?'

'Just to have a look,' he replied. 'It's supposed to be nice. It's the Apple Isle.'

'I've seen apples. If I could afford a holiday, I'd go somewhere where they have things I haven't seen.'

'It wouldn't cost much,' Geoffrey argued. 'We could drive there.'

'You mean I could drive there.' Geoffrey didn't own a car and caught the bus most places.

'They have a boat that ferries cars across. It costs ... $55 per vehicle under two tons. That's a bargain. How much does your car weigh?'

'Why would I know how much my car weighs?'

'Right. Hang on.' He typed something into AltaVista and waited patiently.

This was before Google was a thing. Or wi-fi. We had to plug a box into the telephone, run a cable to the computer, edit scripts so they would work with the box, try several different PPP settings, unplug the cables, plug them back in …

'We've got two flashing green lights on the modem now, what did you do?'

'I changed 255.255.182.4 to 255.255.182.5. Hang on, I'll try 255.255.182.6.'

'Three flashing green lights!'

'What do the flashing lights mean?'

'I'm not sure but three has to be better than two. Try changing it to 255.255.182.7 … no, they're all off now.'

Nowadays, everyone has Google on their phone and they can research information anywhere. It's practically impossible to make things up anymore without someone calling you out.

'Did you know that the word "hike" originally comes from the time when the husband would ride on a mule while the wife had to walk alongside? As the routes were unpaved and muddy, the wife would have to "hike" up her skirt.'

'That's not true. Google says it comes from the old German word "hyke" meaning "to walk vigorously".'

'Okay,' said Geoffrey, 'it says here that a Fiat 124 Coupé weighs 2205 pounds. That's around a ton. Even with our bags it will be well under the weight limit.'

'I doubt the Fiat would make it that far,' I said. 'It's only running on three cylinders and the radiator is shot.'

'I'll pay for your car to be fixed, and we can go halves in petrol. Motels are only about $30 per night if you're not fussy about sleeping arrangements. If we go for a week the entire holiday will only cost a few hundred dollars. It will be a road trip.'

'You'll pay to have my car fixed?'

'Yes.'

'I don't actually have any assignments due.'

'Excellent.'

The drive from Adelaide to Melbourne, where we had to catch the ferry, took just over fourteen hours. It's an eight-hour drive, but we had to keep stopping to top up the radiator. Geoffrey's idea of paying to have the car fixed had consisted of purchasing a bottle of Wynn's Radiator Stop Leak and a new set of wiper blades.

'If we're going to be touring the Apple Isle by car, we want a clean windshield to look out of. You don't have to pay me back for those. They were only $4.'

As we missed the ferry by five hours and had to rebook for the next day, we spent that night in the ferry car park.

When the movie *The Mask* first came out, someone had told Geoffrey that he did an excellent impression of the bit where Jim Carrey says, 'Smokin'!' Since then, he'd wanted to be a voiceover artist, convinced that his repertoire of Fred Flintstone, Crocodile Dundee and John Cleese impressions were nothing short of a gift for others to experience. It was a very long night.

'This parrot is dead! He's an ex-parrot. Bereft of life.'

'Yes, I've seen it, Geoffrey.'

'No, you're meant to say, "He's just resting."'

'Can't we play I-spy instead?'

'Fine. I'll go first. I spy with my little eye, something beginning with an F.'

'Well it's certainly not a ferry.'

'No, but it's got the word ferry in it.'

'What?'

'Yes, it's got three words.'

'That's a sentence.'

'No, it's a name. Of a place.'

'Fuck that then, I'm not playing anymore. What was it?'

'Ferry Booking Office.'

'I'm really tempted to drive the car off the edge of the dock right now and drown us both. What's the time?'

'11.15, so ...' He counted off fingers, 'eighteen hours and fifteen minutes until we get to board. You know what we should do?'

'What?'

'Hum parts of a song and the other person has to guess what the song is.'

'I'm going to go to sleep.'

'Oh, no, don't do that. Then I'll be awake by myself and there's nothing to do. Come on, I'll start. Hmmm hmmm, hmm, hmmm hmmm hmm, hmm.'

'"Bohemian Rhapsody"?'

'No. It didn't sound anything like "Bohemian Rhapsody". You must be tone-deaf. Here, I'll do it again. Hmm hmm, hmmm, hmm hmm hmm.'

'That sounded completely different from the first time.'

'That's because I did a different bit. That was the chorus. I'd have thought you'd get it easy with the chorus. Do you want me to hum it again?'

'No, I give it up. What was it?'

'"Don't You Want Me" by The Human League.'

'What time is it now?'

'11.18.'

At 4.30pm the next day, we were first in line to drive aboard.

The ship was essentially a floating parking deck. Due to the booking change, the only tickets available were 'Ocean Recliner', which meant sitting in a chair overnight with no shower facilities after our thirty-six hours in the car.

A few chairs down from us, a couple had a child with a toothache and a set of healthy lungs, but we managed to get a few minutes of sleep regardless. We drove off the ship into Devonport at six the next morning, leaving a large puddle of coolant behind.

Devonport looked a lot like Adelaide, and I had never been that impressed with Adelaide. We filled the radiator and headed south. Our original five-day plan had been to tour the island in a clockwise route, with overnight stays in Launceston, Hobart, Queenstown and Burnie, before arriving back in Devonport for departure. We'd already missed our first night, so we made the decision to bypass Launceston and head straight to Hobart instead.

'We should stop and buy apples,' declared Geoffrey. We were driving through farming land and, every few kilometres, kiosks selling apples were set up at the front of properties.

'Why?' I asked.

'We're in the Apple Isle. We have to buy apples. Tasmania is famous for them. People will ask us about the apples when we get back, and what are you going to tell them? That we didn't try any? That's just ridiculous.'

'I'm fairly certain they are the same apples we buy in Adelaide. All our apples come from here.'

'Yes, but these ones haven't been in a truck. And a boat. They're straight off the trees. Besides, we need snacks for the road trip. Pull over at this one.'

Geoffrey purchased two large bags from the vendor, a woman with no teeth who told us we were going in the wrong direction. We headed back the way we had come, looking for the turn-off.

'Do you want one?' Geoffrey offered the bag to me.

'No, thanks.'

'You're not even going to try one?'

'I kind of like the green ones better. They're more crisp.'

'These are pretty crisp,' Geoffrey replied. 'Listen ...' He took a large bite.

'I stand corrected. That did indeed sound crisp.'

'Do you want one, then?'

'No, thanks.'

'Fine. All the more apples for me. I'm fairly sure that was the turn-off, by the way.'

'What?'

'You missed the turn-off.'

'Well why didn't you tell me it was coming up?'

'You're the one driving.'

'Yes, and you're the navigator,' I countered. 'That's your job. You have the map.'

During our trip across on the ferry, we'd taken time out from our designated chairs to eat at the cafeteria. It was slim pickings – pre-wrapped sandwiches and the like – and we had to line up with trays like they make you do at IKEA. Our tray liners, A3 pieces of paper, featured an outline of Tasmania, with landmarks, for kids to colour in with a supplied small box of crayons. The crayons, four per box, were only slightly thicker than a piece of wire, and one of them was white. They kept snapping and were constructed from a material not unlike crayon, but not similar enough to leave much of a mark on paper. Our proposed route was marked in purple crayon, with tourist locations we intended to visit coloured in green. Geoffrey had also shaded the shoreline in with blue.

'The map doesn't show the turn-off. It just has a picture of a turtle. I'm going by what the old lady told me. She said to turn left at the big rock shaped like a boot. That road will take us to a main road that goes all the way to Hobart.'

'Was there a rock shaped like a boot?'

'Kind of.'

'Right. I'll keep going for a bit then, and if we don't see a rock that is definitely shaped like a boot, we'll head back.'

'No, it was definitely boot-shaped.'

I turned the car around and drove back. The rock wasn't shaped anything like a boot.

'Maybe you misunderstood because of her thick Tasmanian accent and lack of teeth.'

'No,' Geoffrey replied. 'She definitely said "boot". Maybe it depends on which angle you look at it from.'

'It's round. Whatever angle you look at it from, it's going to be round. Perhaps you should have asked her what kind of boot: a boot-shaped one or the round kind.'

'It's not perfectly round – it has a bit that sticks up at the back. I can definitely see a kind of boot shape.'

We took the turn-off. It led to a farmhouse, so we reversed back down their driveway and continued on along the highway until we found the correct landmark. It was actually shaped like a boot. Someone had spray-painted black laces on it. Someone else had spray-painted the words 'Ken Matthews is a wanker' in white.

'Oh, yes,' said Geoffrey, 'I saw that when we drove past earlier.'

'You knew where the boot was?'

'It didn't register that it was boot-shaped at the time. I was too busy wondering who Ken Matthews is and if he has seen that rock. He would have been pretty cross.'

On the five-hour drive to Hobart, Geoffrey made me play a game that he invented called 'Number Plate People'. As cars drove past us, we had to record the letters and numerals from their number plate and use each letter as the first letters of someone's name. GZA-426, for example, became Glen Zoe Alice. The numbers indicated the probability of the person driving the car being called Glen, Zoe or Alice. In this case, a four in twenty-six chance. It was far more excruciating than I am making it sound.

'Losing that day has really mucked up our schedule,' Geoffrey complained as he marked our new route on the map. He'd tried colouring over the old route with the white crayon but it hadn't worked. He held it up. 'Ignore everything in purple. Everything green is where we are going now. Except the green whale.'

'Right, well you're the navigator. We've already established your skills in that area.'

'Okay, because we lost a day, and it's now nearly noon on Sunday, we should turn left up here. That will take us to Port Arthur.'

'What's at Port Arthur?'

'It's the ruins of an old prison.'

'Oh, good. I thought we were going straight to Hobart, but visiting ruins sounds much better than food and a shower.'

'We can eat at Port Arthur,' Geoffrey replied. 'They have a cafe. If we go to Hobart first, we won't have time to get there before the prison closes, and I will have to colour over it with purple. I know how long it takes you to shower.'

When I was growing up, my father had very strict water usage rules. If using the sink, under no circumstances were we to use the hot tap. If using the shower, we were not to exceed three minutes. He would set a timer, and if the water was still on when the buzzer went off, he'd barge into the bathroom yelling and turn it off. He was a bit of a dick. As the shower took a few minutes to warm up, we had to lather ourselves with soap and shampoo outside the stream and use the remaining sixty seconds to wash it off. After my father left us, everyone took as long as they fucking wanted in the shower. Since then, my showers have extended to two, sometimes three hours. I usually turn on the shower and make a coffee while waiting for it to get nice and steamy. Then I get in and have my coffee with a cigarette. After enjoying the water for a while, I shave, brush my teeth, shampoo my hair and wash. In that order, but the time between each varies. Then I enjoy the water for a while. Sometimes I try to drown a bug or see how much water I can hold with my arms crossed or hold my arms down with my fingers splayed to make the water run off the tips. My current bathroom has a television and coffee machine in it. I tried putting a beanbag in the shower but, after a few months, the stitching rotted away and it burst, so now I use a camping chair.

The Port Arthur Historical Site was an hour out of our way. Geoffrey suggested we continue our game of Number Plate People, and I threatened to swerve into oncoming traffic.

'Let's play Science Fiction Movies then. I'll say a science fiction movie, and whatever letter it ends with, you have to name a science fiction movie that starts with that letter.'

'Righto,' I agreed, '*Star Wars*.'

'No, I go first.'

'Okay.'

'*Star Wars*.'

'Really? Fine. *Star Wars: The Empire Strikes Back*.'

'No, you can't use *Star Wars* twice in a row.'

'Are you just saying that because you can't think of a science fiction film that starts with K?' I asked.

'No.'

'Fine, *Spaceballs* then.'

'That's really more of a comedy than science fiction, but I'll let you have it. *Star Wars: The Empire Strikes Back*.'

'Right, I'm not playing anymore.'

'Oh, come on.'

'No. I wouldn't have thought it possible ten minutes ago, but you actually managed to come up with a game more painful than Number Plate People.'

'Let's play Animals then.'

'Do you name an animal and I use the last letter to name another animal?'

'No, I make an animal sound and you have to guess what it is. I'll go first. *Araack!*'

'That just sounded like someone yelling the name "Eric". Is it Eric's mother?'

'No, it's *Araack!*, not "Eric". I'll give you a clue: it's brown.'

'That's not much of a clue. Most animals are brown.'

'Yes, but only one of them says *Araack!*'

'Is it a camel?'

'No.'

'I give up then. What was it?'

'Oh, don't give up yet,' Geoffrey moaned. 'I'll give you one more clue. It has long eyelashes.'

'That's all I get to go on? It's brown, has long eyelashes, and yells "Eric"?'

'*Araack!*'

'Right, well I don't give a fuck what it is, it sounds dreadful.'

'It was a seal.'

'It didn't sound anything like a seal. Seals bark.'

'No, that's dogs. Because you didn't get it, I get to go again. *Braaad!*'

We arrived and drove through a tollbooth and into the car park just after 1pm. It was a nice day, warm with blue skies and a light breeze. There were quite a few tourists. Geoffrey consulted the brochure that we had been given at the ticket office.

'What do you want to look at first? The prison ruins or the church ruins?'

'Where's the cafe?' I asked.

Geoffrey consulted the brochure again. It had a little map on the back. He pointed to a building.

'That's the gift shop and cafe,' he said, 'but we should look at the ruins first. I'm not really all that hungry.'

'Really? You only ate two bags of apples. You don't want a barrel of plums or a bucket of apricots to go with them? I'm going to get something to eat.'

We made our way up the steps of the building and entered through the gift shop. I bought a black-and-white striped T-shirt with 'Inmate of Port Arthur Prison' printed on it. Geoffrey bought a coffee mug and a fridge magnet.

The cafe had the IKEA tray system, so we grabbed a tray each and made our way down the line. I had my eye on a cherry danish, but the man in front of us took it.

'Good choice,' I said. 'I was going to get that.'

The man turned and frowned. He had blond wavy hair, parted in the middle, and was carrying a big bag.

'You can have it if you like. It's burnt on the edges. I don't like them when they are overcooked.'

He offered the danish to me.

'No, no. You enjoy your cherry danish. I'm sure it will be delicious, despite the burnt edges.'

'I don't mind.'

'I'll have it then,' said Geoffrey. He took the danish.

The man with the blond wavy hair and I each selected a slice of carrot cake instead.

'Snap,' I said.

'What?'

'Snap. You know, the card game.'

'No. Is it like Uno?'

'Not really.'

'It's more like Go Fish,' Geoffrey interjected helpfully.

'No, it's not,' I told the man with blond wavy hair. 'Don't listen to him. He's insane.'

'It's for the same age group,' Geoffrey argued.

'Right, so by that argument, Slip'N Slide is also similar to Snap.'

'I've never played Slip Inside, so I wouldn't know,' said Geoffrey. 'Is it like Go Fish?'

'Are you serious? Slip'N Slide. The long piece of yellow plastic that you put on your lawn, spray water on, and kids slide down.'

'Oh, you mean the Splash'N Ride?'

'What the fuck? Who calls it the Splash'N Ride?'

'That's what the one we had was called.'

'You must have had a cheap Chinese knock-off then. The real one is called Slip'N Slide. Where'd you get it?'

'I'm not sure. Maybe Target. Can you pass me one of those

splades please?'

Further up the line, I added a cheese sandwich and a bag of chips to my tray. Geoffrey selected a banana to 'mix things up a bit'. I have no idea what the man with the blond wavy hair added, because Geoffrey and I were busy arguing about whether the plastic spoons with a built-in fork were called splades or sporks. We paid for our meal and made our way outside to eat on the balcony. Wasps hovered near an open bin by the door, so I carried on a bit and we sat at a table towards the back. I'm not a fan of wasps.

Once, when I was young, my family drove up the coast to stay at a beachside town called Kalbarri during summer break. We rented a cabin at the Kalbarri Caravan Park. On the beach, there was a small shack that rented out snorkelling equipment, so my sister and I hurriedly searched through bags for our swimming outfits. My father walked around with his hands on his hips, nodding and commenting on what an excellent choice in accommodation he had made.

'Look, ceiling fans. Very nice. The ceiling appears to be bowing here, though, and there's a stain in the middle that looks wet.'

He reached up on tippy-toes and poked the wet spot with his finger. His finger went straight through, opening a hole about an inch in diameter. Wasps poured out of the hole. Thousands of them. The room looked like yellow and black static. Everyone was stung multiple times, but my father took the brunt of the attack. After he was released from hospital, my mother had to drive the car home because my father couldn't open his eyes due to the swelling. It was the third-worst holiday I have ever been on.

The man with the blond wavy hair sat a few tables down from us. He smiled and raised his spork with a bit of carrot cake on it in way of a salute.

'They're not European wasps, so you don't have to worry,' he said.

'Sorry?'

'Those are just normal wasps. There's a lot of wasps about today, but I haven't seen any European wasps.'

'What's the difference?' Geoffrey asked, seemingly quite interested. 'Is there a noticeable size or colour variation?'

The man with the blond wavy hair seemed pleased at this engagement.

'They're the same colour, but European wasps are smaller than normal wasps. They look more like bees. A man came to our house and hung European wasp traps on the trees in our backyard because our neighbour had a nest of them in their shed. I looked in one, and it was full of dead European wasps. We've got lots of European wasps in Tasmania, but those,' he indicated towards the bin, 'are just yellow paper wasps. They won't kill you.'

'Well that's good to hear,' said Geoffrey. 'You certainly know a lot about wasps.'

'That's because I'm a wasp scientist,' said the man with the blond wavy hair. 'That's my job.'

'Really?' I asked. 'Why didn't you put the traps on the trees yourself then?'

Geoffrey kicked my leg under the table.

'It's a valid question,' I continued. 'Had you run out of your own wasp traps? As you're a wasp scientist, it might be assumed that you'd have an abundant supply.'

'So,' said Geoffrey, attempting to change the subject, 'you live around here? That must be nice.'

'Apart from all the wasps, of course,' I added. 'You'll probably be on top of that, though, once you get some more traps.'

Geoffrey kicked me again.

The man with the blond wavy hair nodded. 'Are you from the mainland?'

'Yes,' Geoffrey answered, finishing the last bite of his banana. 'Adelaide. It's a shithole.'

Adelaide isn't a shithole. It has some nice bits. It's the people who live in Adelaide that ruin it. Seen as a kind of joke by the rest of Australia, Adelaidians spend a lot of their time trying to convince themselves, and other Adelaidians, that they are not a joke and are actually fairly damn awesome. This means dressing in the latest European fashions, even just to visit the supermarket, and pretending they spend a lot of time in Melbourne and Sydney. Adelaide is more like a large village than a city. A village where the idiots outnumber normal townsfolk a hundred to one, and they all wear G-Star and Diesel. The tourism slogan for Adelaide is: 'It's heaps good.'

I wish I was making this up.

We left our trays on a counter near the bins, dodged a few wasps, and wandered down a grassy hill towards the ruins. Behind us, the man with the blond wavy hair finished his meal and carried his big bag back inside the cafe.

'I've never met a wasp scientist before,' I said to Geoffrey. 'I certainly learned a lot.'

'He seemed harmless enough,' Geoffrey replied. 'You have to expect Tasmanians to be a little odd. They don't have much to do apart from growing apples, so they probably get a bit bored and make up stories to sound more interesting. Stand on top of that rock, and I'll take a photo.'

When I was nine, I told a kid at school that I was having a birthday party and he could come if he wanted. It was nowhere near my birthday, I just made the whole thing up. The kid was kind of a bully, and I thought that by inviting him, he would direct his attention towards others. Word quickly got around and, cornered by the lie, I confirmed to around twenty kids that yes, I was having a birthday party, and yes, they could come. I was enjoying the attention at this stage. To add realism, I gave each kid a sheet from a pad of party invites with my address and a date set weeks in the future, figuring this would give me enough time to think of a way out of the whole thing. I forgot all about it until the first guests arrived. My father was watching cricket on television while my mother was out doing the weekly shopping.

'I'll stand next to it,' I said to Geoffrey. 'There's no point standing on it. People are watching.'

'Just stand on it,' he replied. 'How is standing next to a rock even remotely interesting? We should make it our theme.'

'Our theme?'

'Yes, the theme of our holiday photos. We stand on a rock in every shot. Oh, no ...'

'What?'

'We should have got a photo standing on the rock shaped like a boot.'

'Yes,' I agreed, 'and the round one.'

Geoffrey frowned. 'No, that would be stupid.'

I stood on the rock.

'Okay,' Geoffrey queried, 'is that what you are going to do? Just stand there? You don't want to pretend you're doing something?'

'Like what?'

'I don't know, pointing at something, perhaps.'

'No, just take the photo.'

'What if you jumped with your arms in the air?'

'Like an action shot?'

'Yes, exactly.'

'No, just take the photo.'

Inside the cafe, the man with the blond wavy hair unzipped his big bag, took out an AR-15 semiautomatic assault rifle, and began shooting patrons and staff.

'Gunshots!' exclaimed Geoffrey. 'We're missing a re-enactment. I bet a convict has escaped and the prison wardens are chasing him. Let's go watch.'

'It's coming from way up the hill,' I replied. 'We just came from there. They will probably do another one in an hour. Let's just finish looking at rocks and then we can walk back up. It sounds like it's finished anyway.'

The man with the blond wavy hair reloaded the assault rifle and stepped out of the cafe. Tourists heading towards the area hoping to catch part of a re-enactment were fired upon.

'No,' said Geoffrey. 'Listen, it's still going. Quick, take a photo of me standing on the rock and then we'll go watch.'

Geoffrey climbed onto the rock, looked to his left and held his hand to his forehead.

'Why are you saluting?' I asked.

'I'm not,' he replied. 'I'm gazing into the distance. Just hurry up and take the shot. We're missing the re-enactment.'

'Okay.' I took the photo. 'Now, put your hands on your knees, bend them a little, turn to the side a bit, a bit more, and put your head back and smile ...'

'You really are a dickhead,' Geoffrey said, jumping down.

We were halfway back up the hill when an old lady came running down past us. She was a large woman with blue eye shadow, a tight perm and tighter white slacks. Both her knees had large green grass stains where she had fallen and skidded.

'Run!' she screamed.

We ran. The look on her face as she yelled her warning was all the convincing we needed.

'Is it zombies?' Geoffrey yelled as we passed her.

Many hours later, after police officers took our statements and contact information, we were free to leave. We hadn't been anywhere near the cafe during the shootings, so could provide no helpful eyewitness accounts. There was no discussion about driving back to Devonport – I just drove there. Both of us wanted to be home.

'I hope the wasp guy is alright,' said Geoffrey.

'I'm sure he's fine,' I said. 'I didn't see him ... you know.'

Geoffrey nodded. 'They were covered, though. It was pretty hard to tell. Some of the sheets were small ...'

'Do you want to play Number Plate People?' I asked.

'Alright.'

From Look Evelyn, Duck Dynasty Wiper Blades.
We Should Get Them. *by David Thorne (27b/6 2014)*

ANNABEL CRABB

The Wife Drought

❛Why am I writing this peering round an infant who is intently stuffing Cheerios up my nose? I want a wife, damn it. And I don't see how all these bozos get one, when I don't.❜

It was a funny sort of setting for a personal light-bulb moment. I was interstate at a 'summit' – one of those networking events at which various professionals and public policy experts waft about, politely waiting for each other to finish before sharing their own views. I was already in a bit of an ill temper about it. Having accepted the invitation to attend, I belatedly opened the conference programme and immediately experienced a familiar, sinking feeling as I scanned the columns and columns of male names – economists, business figures, foreign policy experts – and realised that I had very likely been invited to chock up the event's skirt-rate.

All the signs were there. The morning involved a series of panels in which the panellists were all blokes, and my job – as moderator – was to provide some sort of perky connective tissue. I noticed with particular horror that the following day I was scheduled to cross-examine, for sixty minutes, a chap who was a world expert in some sort of climatology in which I was significantly less expert. Of course, these things usually turn out to be interesting and worthwhile, and so indeed did this one, but as I headed to lunch on that first day I could not quite subdue the plaintive little voice in the back of my skull asking why I had abandoned my children for this.

As luck would have it, I ran into an old pal at lunch: a fellow who had been a ministerial adviser in Canberra, but was now doing less, for more, in the private sector. We exchanged enthusiastic greetings and sat down. 'What's new with you?' I asked.

'I'm married! And we have a toddler!' he announced. Much mutual agreement ensued about how lovely children are, and so on.

'Yes, life is great,' he continued, digging with gusto into his French-trimmed lamb cutlets. 'My wife has quit her job, so I can be absolutely confident our child's getting the best of care. It's all worked out really well.'

Now, I like this bloke. I really do. And I wish him nothing but happiness. But why did I suddenly want to push his smiling face into the potatoes dauphinoise? Was it just because I was in a huff after spending the morning trying to make a group of economists sound interesting, while back in Sydney my own children nosed through rubbish bins for sustenance?

It's all worked out really well. I looked around the room, and I recognised what was going on. How many of these blokes had wives at home – picking up kids from school, digging Play-Doh out of the cracks in the floorboards for the gazillionth time, taking Nanna to the doctor, waiting around for the phone guy to turn up 'between the hours of eight and twelve', which, as any veteran of the game will tell you, actually means 'thirty seconds after you have disappeared round the corner for a quick sortie to school to deliver the lunch bag that was left on the table this morning'.

The hour of 2.45pm would never, for these men, bring that faint but always perceptible neural pressure. They had wives. I looked at the women I could see in the room. Was it my imagination or did they look kind of distracted?

I glanced back at my companion, chomping obliviously through his delicious lunch. He didn't even realise how fortunate he was; what a lucky door prize he'd won. What a weird and – for him – wonderful crimp in the sociological evolution of humanity it was that allowed him to walk out the door at 8am, work a full and rewarding day, eat a nice lunch with both his hands, and come home – or so I imagined – to a newly bathed baby poised for bed.

He thought that was just how things worked. And the worst thing of all? He was right. Men get wives, and women don't. That *is* how it works.

I had wife envy, and I had it bad.

Bouts of wife envy strike me periodically. Sometimes it happens in airports, where I see squads of booming businessmen flocking together into the Qantas Club, while I am skulking by, possibly with a nipper strapped to my chest who has just observed the baby's prerogative to go what Martin Amis once termed 'super-void' in an already spongy nappy just as the final call sign starts flashing. The resultant reproachful personal paging and walk of shame onto the flight, to be confronted by the politely horrified eyes of my seat neighbour, only exacerbates my envy. 'Well, yes,' I want to say to the guy I'm sitting next to. 'I find this a bit confronting as well, just so you know.'

I, too, want to go over that report while enjoying a complimentary Crown Lager. I, too, want to talk genially about what a little tiger my young son is, while peacefully completing my meeting presentation, safe in the knowledge that his every need is being met by my beautiful wife. Why am I writing this peering round an infant who is intently stuffing Cheerios up my nose? I want a wife, damn it. And I don't see how all these bozos get one, when I don't.

If you are working full-time, and your spouse is working either part-time or not at all, then – congratulations! You have a 'wife'. A wife, traditionally, is a person who pulls back on paid work in order to do more of the unpaid work that accumulates around the home (cleaning, fixing stuff, being around for when the plumber doesn't turn up, spending a subsequent hour on hold to find out why the plumber didn't turn up, and so on). This sort of work goes into overdrive once you add children to the equation, and the list of household jobs grows exponentially to include quite specialised work such as raising respectful, pleasant young people, and getting stains off things with a paste of vinegar and sodium bicarbonate.

A 'wife' can be male or female. Whether they're men or women, though, the main thing wives are is a cracking professional asset. They enable the busy full-time worker to experience the joy and fulfilment of children, without the considerable inconvenience of having to pick them up from school at 3pm, which – in one of the human experience's wittier little jokes – is the time that school ends, a time that is convenient for pretty much no one. Having a wife means that if you get caught up at work, or want to stay later, either to get some urgent job finished or to frown at your desktop computer in a plausible simulacrum of working in order to impress a new boss while actually reading BuzzFeed, it can be done. Many wives work, but they do jobs that are either part-time or offer sufficient flexibility for the accommodation of late-breaking debacles.

In the olden days, wives were usually women. Which is funny, because nowadays wives are usually women too.

I first started thinking seriously about the significance of wives back in 2013, when Tony Abbott named a federal Cabinet with only one woman in it, and the nation went into one of its periodic fits of self-examination as to why there aren't more women in federal politics. I wrote a column expressing my view that if women MPs were blessed with wives in the same way that male MPs frequently are, you might get quite a noticeable participatory uptick, because that way women wouldn't have to choose between having a career in politics and having a family. Many women have had to do that over the years, while male politicians breed like hamsters while in office and nobody even notices.

I was left in no doubt, by the resultant stream of correspondence, that asymmetric rates of wife-having are a disparity not restricted to MPs. Businesswomen, executives, academics, journalists and lawyers wrote to me with spookily similar experiences. All of them watched their male contemporaries and competitors start families, and noticed how fatherhood made barely any difference to the way those guys worked; they still worked long hours, travelled at the drop of a hat, or had no difficulty making work functions after-hours. Usually it was because they had wives who either stayed at home full-time or worked fewer hours in order to manage child care. But my correspondents didn't have wives, and all of them thought life would be easier if they did.

Right then, I thought. Just out of curiosity, how many working fathers have 'wives' in Australia, compared to working mothers? What exactly, in other words, is the comparative national rate of wife-having, expressed as a ratio between women and men? Ascertaining how many working dads have part-time or stay-at-home partners, compared to the other way around, should be a relatively easy business, I assumed. Surely some statistics nut must have had a gander at it at some stage.

My search for this information began blithely, with a few confident Google key-strokes, but quickly degenerated into a horrifying snarl-up involving the 2011 Census data, much back-of-the-envelope calculation, reams and reams of almost-helpful Australian Bureau of Statistics tables, and some heroic assumptions on my part that would offend any serious statistician. There was plenty of data on fathers' employment, and mothers' employment. But that was no use to me; I wanted to join them together, and find out which dads and which mums lived together, and how they managed things between them.

Eventually, I did what many a statistical fraud would do in my position: I telephoned the Australian Institute of Family Studies, and asked to speak to Jennifer Baxter. I didn't know Jenny, but her name was on all the most interesting reports I'd read about patterns in male and female employment, especially in relation to families. If anyone could yank the figures I was after, I was fairly confident it would be Jenny. And when I finally ran her to earth, after dealing with the traditional public-relations maze that most agencies have now installed to shield their employees from the horror of journalists cold-calling them, she was pleasantly receptive.

I explained my problem: what I really wanted was a wife-count. Who had wives? Was it still just a bloke thing? Or were ladies getting them too these days?

Jenny was exceedingly helpful, and her voice had the rich, reassuring cadence of the supernumerate. Just as I'd hoped. But she warned me not to get too excited. 'I get a lot of journalists ringing me about stay-at-home dads,' she said, kindly. 'Everybody wants a story about how they're on the rise. But they're not, really. You look at the data, and it's just not there.'

A day or two later, Jenny emailed me an exciting little package of data, which she had tickled out of the 2011 Census data with the assistance of her data-crunching software and her brain; always likely to be a better bet, I guess, than *my* brain, a pencil and forty-eight cups of tea, which is what I'd used.

And here's the story. Of Australian couple families with kids under the age of fifteen, 60 per cent have a dad who works full-time, and a mum who works either part-time or not at all. How many families have a mum who works full-time, and a dad who is at home or works part-time? Three per cent.

Who gets wives? Dads do. Most mums have to make do with alternative arrangements. Only one in four mothers with children under the age of fifteen work full-time. These are the women who – in all sorts of lines of work – find themselves in open competition in the full-time workplace. What interests me is: how do their circumstances compare against the dads who are doing similar jobs? How many of the full-time working mothers have 'wives', compared with the full-time working dads?

It turns out that in Australian workplaces, 76 per cent of full-time working dads have a 'wife'. Three out of four. But among the mothers who work full-time, the rate of wife-having is much, much lower: only 15 per cent.

Working fathers, in other words, are five times as likely to have a 'wife' as working mothers. As I suspected: Australian working women are in an advanced, sustained and chronically under-reported state of wife drought, and there is no sign of rain.

I think of a *Candid Camera* show I once saw, where applicants for a job in a doughnut factory were told they needed to do a trial shift on the boxing line. Secretly filmed, the candidates donned their hairnets and sat down at a conveyor belt, stacking freshly made doughnuts neatly into boxes. But as they worked, the conveyor belt got faster and faster. The piles of doughnuts got messier and messier as the poor victims tried to keep up. Eventually, they were just chucking the things into the boxes any which way, as more and more doughnuts relentlessly poured forth from the maw of the machine. It was – in the classic manner of such TV shows – utterly unbearable to watch.

That segment summarises to me what juggling work and family feels like. You start off alright, and all your doughnuts are going where they are supposed to go. But as more jobs materialise, and more deadlines bob up, and freakishly unexpected developments arrive (your child comes down with gastro; the hot water tap in the bathroom inexplicably gets jammed at full bore; your boss announces that now would be a good time for you to deliver a formal progress report on your project to the board; suddenly the prime minister's on the TV announcing a snap Royal Commission into something; everyone gets nits), everything has to be done just that little bit faster, and the faster you go the more the panic rises, as does the guilt about doing everything just that little bit worse. You're just hurling the damn doughnuts now, hating doughnuts and wondering why anyone would ever bother eating the stupid things anyway. Generally, it's at this point that you'll realise that you forgot it was your mother's birthday yesterday. Or you'll stub your toe, and dissolve into a wail of entirely disproportionate self-pity.

It's not just about the work hours involved. Paid work can be demanding, stressful and exacting. But work in the home can consume a huge amount of emotional bandwidth, in which failure brings a sense of guilt and self-recrimination far more tearing and existential than what you feel when you bugger something up mildly at work.

For example: I am fast approaching the deadline for finishing this book. In the past twelve weeks, I've written eighty thousand words. In the weeks to come, there are dense weeks of parliamentary drama, the planning of a new *Kitchen Cabinet* series, several speeches and God knows what else. But the only thing that has actually reduced me to tears is Chiquita, a foot-tall stuffed kangaroo.

Chiquita lives at the childcare centre my four-year-old son attends twice a week. Every holiday, a lucky child gets to take Chiquita home and show her a good time. Chiquita travels with her own scrapbook, and the idea is that parents will capture action shots of Chiquita's adventures with her juvenile escort, then paste them into the book to create a permanent marsupial travel diary. At Easter, it was our turn.

Chiquita had a quiet holiday. We forgot to take her to the Easter Show. We forgot to take her to the pool. We forgot to take her to the museum. Any outing we actually achieved was undertaken in Chiquita's absence; she spent most of Easter perched hopefully on the dinner table. It was only at the eleventh hour of the Easter egg hunt, when the children were half-heartedly poking through undergrowth for any overlooked goodies, that anyone remembered to get a snap of Chiquita even vaguely near the action. The day before Chiquita was due back, the task of printing out the lame Chiquita pictures drummed at the back of my skull. I had a column and two speeches to write. Three o'clock was fast approaching. I had just enough time to get to the photo shop, if I hustled. The discovery that the photo shop had gone out of business the day before very nearly finished me. With Herculean restraint, I did not actually claw hysterically at the expressionless roller door securing the defunct shop's dim interior. But I wanted to.

Sticking pictures of a nomadic stuffed kangaroo in a book is – in economic terms – an insignificant piece of work, of no interest to national productivity, immaterial to the formal prosperity of my household. But the emotional exposure is considerable, and this is at the heart of the Chiquita Syndrome: I do not want my son to be the kid who brings the Chiquita book back blank because his mum was too busy to organise it. Failing Chiquita isn't like failing as an employee; it feels like failing as a person, which cuts much deeper, notwithstanding the triviality of the enterprise itself.

Chiquita is a small but typical example of 'wife work' – utterly invisible to the national economy, but significant to the wellbeing of a family. She fits beautifully into the job specifications for the position of 'wife', which might look something like this:

Opening exists for leader of a small, spirited team in a vibrant but often chaotic environment. Applicant must be mature and patient, as team members may at times be prone to sudden mood swings, unorthodox social techniques, strategic tunnel vision and outright insubordination.

Applicant will have responsibility for cleaning, laundering, tutoring, light maintenance, heavy maintenance, procurement, occupational health and safety, occupational therapy, nutrition, ethical guidance counselling, transport, skills training, intra-team human resource management, out-sourcing, mentoring, mediation, education and sanitation.

Fine motor control and calm temperament a must. Creative experience and demonstrated innovation strong advantages, esp. capacity to construct, for example, a plausible bat costume from basic household items in under ten minutes.

Some tasks may be repetitive. Formal performance assessment very limited, though applicant may self-assess regularly in bleaker moments.

Salary nominal.

If you look at this gig through the eyes of a conventional jobseeker, it's pretty obvious why blokes do not regularly apply. The signposts of success in the workplace – the clear milestones and targets, the achievement of which might earn you backslaps or bonuses or both – are nowhere to be seen. You don't get paid, which I guess is sort of a deal-breaker for some people straight up. Achievements may frequently prove fleeting, and soon forgotten. Washed clothes get dirty again. A perfectly balanced, home-cooked dinner still gets eaten, and will encounter exactly the same digestive fate as frozen pizza. Toys, blocks and general filth will quickly reclaim any territory cleared by even quite concerted parental effort. Some of the key performance indicators – looking at you, Chiquita – are so random as to be ridiculous.

If you do well at this job, the returns are hugely significant: good relationships with your children, a balanced approach to life, probably a happy retirement in which you will be able to enjoy yourself with gentle pursuits, rather than working till you're seventy and then dropping dead. But we're talking some pretty long-tail business there. In the meantime maybe someone will thank you for it. Or maybe they won't.

From The Wife Drought *by Annabel Crabb*
(Random House Australia 2014)

SHAUN MICALLEF

Trying Too
Hard Now

‘The movie screening that night was *Rambo III*. Everyone enjoyed themselves, except for Rocky. He was completely confused by the film, and the next day he wrote a letter to TriStar Pictures asking about the actor who'd starred in it. He'd missed the name.’

As they drove home in the limo, Rocky seemed distracted. Adrian noticed it, and so did Paulie. The unveiling of the statue hadn't gone well. Rock had tried to announce his retirement, but Clubber Lang had turned up and taunted him, goading him into one more fight – even insulting Adrian. It was Mickey who asked him what was wrong.

Rocky didn't turn from the window. His eyes were fixed on the frozen waters of the Schuylkill. 'It bothers me, Mick,' he said to his manager of many years. 'It bothers me that they were playing that tune, you know.'

Mickey squinted and turned his good ear to the champ. 'What tune, Rock? Whataya talkin' about?'

'You know – that tune the brass band was playin' when they unveiled the statue.'

In the rear-view mirror, Paulie's eyes narrowed and flicked for a moment from the traffic on the Ben Franklin Parkway to meet Adrian's. Both were worried, but Rocky was too troubled to notice. Paulie turned into 19th Street.

Mickey twisted his face more than normal and snarled away the champ's concern. 'You're a fighter, what do you know from music?'

Rocky lowered his eyes and smiled. Perhaps Mickey was right – he *was* just a fighter; a bruiser from Philly who got lucky and wound up on top.

But if Rocky had anything, it was a good gut instinct. He didn't know why, but that music that high school band was playing was just plain WRONG. 'Gonna Fly Now' by Bill Conti. *How would the band even know that piece of music existed?*

A few weeks later, Rocky and Mickey were in the Biltmore Hotel in Los Angeles training for the Clubber Lang bout. Why they'd gone there was a mystery, given the fight was gonna be back in Philly. It was a circus. Autograph hunters, the press, gawkers, geeks and hangers-on. Paulie was in the corner selling merchandise, and a string quartet was playing in the background. When Mickey heard them launch into 'Gonna Fly Now', he swung around and barked at them: 'Shut up, back there, can't you? Change your tune.'

Mickey knew something. Rocky saw it in his eyes. Flinty and scared. Could it be? The little man who'd knocked Ginny Russell out of the ring in '23? The fiery bantamweight with seventy-two wins under his belt and only one loss? Mickey Goldmill – scared?

You bet.

Rocky wanted to talk to him about it, but they had training to do. He'd ask Mickey later. There was plenty of time. On the night of the big fight at the Spectrum, as they were walking through the tunnel on their way to the ring, Rocky was about to mention it, but Mickey mysteriously collapsed and died of a heart attack before he could say anything.

Strange.

A few years later, when Rocky flew back to America after defeating Ivan Drago in Moscow, he was climbing off the plane when the marching band that was there to greet him started playing 'Gonna Fly Now'.

He turned to his wife on the steps behind him. 'Yo, Adrian – you hear that? It's that tune again.' Adrian held his hand tight and told him not to worry about it. 'Yeah, but how can I not worry about it?' he said. 'It's driving me crazy, you know. It's like – it's haunting me or something.' It bothered him so much that he didn't even notice his son was now five or six years older than he had been when he'd left for Russia only a month earlier.

He mentioned the music to his doctors, and they concluded he had brain damage and recommended he never fight again. Paulie told him to shut up about it; that it was causing problems. But Rocky wouldn't listen. He mentioned it to everybody and anybody who'd listen. He even raised it with his accountant, who promised he'd look into it, but then the guy suddenly disappeared – along with all of Rocky's money. He and Adrian and the boy had to move back to Philly; into that dump on Rosehill Street. Paulie got his old job back at the meatworks.

The headaches and blurred vision troubled him a little during his street brawl with Tommy 'The Machine' Gunn in 1990, but he didn't hear that music that year. Maybe he was getting better, he thought. Then the Philadelphia Museum of Art pulled down his statue. They said it wasn't art; that it was 'a movie prop'. What the hell were they talking about? He and Paulie went to talk it out with the museum director, but the guy told them he didn't want to waste his time talking to a pair of fictional characters.

Paulie and Rocky visited the old neighbourhood that night. Mickey's gym on North Front Street, the J&M Tropical Fish store opposite, the Lucky 7 Bar, even his old apartment at 1818 East Tusculum Street. The Atomic Hoagie Shop on the corner of 12th and Cantrell was gone, but the parking lot was still there on Winston Street, just a block away from where he'd walked Little Marie home that night.

Paulie was less sentimental about it all than his brother-in-law. He suggested they get a beer at Andy's and maybe catch a film at the Roxy.

It was late when they left Andy's. Paulie was drunk and insisted on driving the truck. Rocky said okay, but only if they could pick up Spider Rico, Duke Evers and a couple of other old pals on the way. They managed to get to Sansom Street in one piece. It was half an hour until the midnight showing, so the champ left Paulie and the others to get the tickets while he went for a walk through nearby Rittenhouse Park, where Adrian had told him she was pregnant with Rocky Jr.

Back in the lobby, Paulie ran into Tony Gazzo coming out of the men's room. Gazzo warned Paulie that MGM were breathing down his neck, and that Paulie should get the champ to back off and stop asking questions about so-called 'diegetic music' and 'soundtracks'. Paulie tried to reassure him that Rocky would play ball, but Tony was angry. He went a long way back with Rocky and didn't want to see him hurt, he said. Hadn't he looked after Rocky when he was nothing; given him a job as a leg-breaker; some money when he wanted to take out Adrian? Sure, said Paulie, he knew he was a pal. But Gazzo explained he was only a small-time loan shark, and these were the big boys from Hollywood. Paulie said he understood and he'd talk to Rock again. Gazzo said he'd better, and left.

Paulie was waiting out front smoking a cigar when Rocky ambled back from the park. The others had already gone in. 'Listen, we gotta talk, Rocko,' mumbled Paulie.

'Sure, we're talkin' now, ain't we?' joked Rocky, feinting a few jabs and putting his arm around his old friend as they walked back into the lobby. 'But we better get in there; you know how if I miss the first few minutes I don't follow the film so good.'

Paulie lost his temper, as he sometimes did when he was especially drunk or jealous or angry at his sister or fired or around black people. He hurled the half-empty bottle he'd been drinking from at the Rocky pinball machine next to the candy counter. Glass exploded everywhere, and people ran screaming. Paulie was blubbering and begging Rocky to forget about 'that tune' and to stop writing to Bill Conti or they'd both wind up dead. Rocky tried to calm him down, but there was no stopping Paulie once he started feeling sorry for himself. He threw the gold watch Rocky had given him on the floor and kicked it away.

'Oh, Paulie, that's the third one I give you that you gone and broke,' said Rocky, genuinely hurt.

'Just promise me you won't ask no more questions.' Paulie sobbed. 'Please, Rocko.'

Rocky shrugged and looked away and back again for no reason. 'Hey, sure, no problem. All you had to do was ask, you know.'

'Really?' asked Paulie, sniffing back the tears.

'Sure, Paulie,' said Rocky with a smile. 'I'd do anything for you. You're family, right? And there ain't no bustin' up a family.'

The two men embraced, and Paulie wiped his nose on the shoulder of Rocky's jacket. The theatre manager came over to find out what was going on. He was swearing and threatening to throw them both out, but as soon as he saw who it was he apologised for his rudeness and offered them each a complimentary snow cone. Rocky thanked the manager but said that wouldn't be necessary. Paulie said he'd have three, plus a giant bag of popcorn and some Twinkies.

The movie screening that night was *Rambo III*. Everyone enjoyed themselves, except for Rocky. He was completely confused by the film, and the next day he wrote a letter to TriStar Pictures asking about the actor who'd starred in it. He'd missed the name. They never wrote back, but not long afterwards, Adrian mysteriously ended up buried in Laurel Hill Cemetery. No one could recall her dying.

Thirteen years later, Rocky was again jogging through the streets of Philly. Mickey, Apollo Creed and Adrian might have been gone, but the streets out of Kensington remained. The Italian Market, the train tracks off Leigh Avenue, Kelly Drive, over the park bench outside Independence Hall, along the Parkway and up the seventy-seven steps to the eastern plaza of the art museum. He couldn't hear that tune anymore; he couldn't hear anything. If only the patrons of *Rocky: The Musical*, playing at the Winter Garden in New York, had been that lucky.

MONICA DUX

Gone a-Nunning

❛Nuns are meant to be more concerned
with Jesus than with carnal pleasures, yet
Loretta seemed particularly fascinated by
God's naughtier gifts, using the fact that she
taught biology as a convenient cover for
her digressions.❜

Not long after I started high school, my class was told that when we reached Year 10 we'd all get the opportunity to do work experience. My teacher explained that for one week we'd be able to try working in our dream job, just like real grown-ups. To a bunch of twelve-year-olds who had never even heard the words 'wage slave', 'sexual harassment' or 'office Christmas party', work sounded like an entirely thrilling prospect. So when the teacher invited us to take a moment to think about the jobs that we might one day like to try, the rest of the class erupted in excited whispering. I alone sat there in smug silence, for I already knew where my future lay. My burning ambition, my heart's one desire, was to be a nun.

My big mistake was sharing this with Sharon Dunbar. Due to our common alphabetic destiny, Sharon and I sat next to each other in class, but if it wasn't for our surnames I doubt we'd have even made eye contact. She wasn't a mean girl, but she was tough, while I was a certified dag, bookish and awkward. Sharon wore her school dress dangerously short, was known to have pierced her own ears with her mum's sewing needles and had told me all about something called 'dry rooting', which sounded intriguing but very unhygienic.

When it came to work experience, Sharon obviously didn't need to do much thinking either, because she quickly turned to me and announced that she wanted to be a beautician. This wouldn't have surprised anyone, for that very morning Sharon had made fashion ripples at school by turning up with bleached hair. And when I say bleached, I mean it quite literally, in that she'd White Kinged herself, attacking her unfortunate scalp with the same stuff her mum used to whiten the Dunbar sheets.

Emboldened by Sharon's career-related confidence, I confided right back at her, admitting that my dream was to become a bride of Christ. Did she think that would be allowed? I fully understood how serious the nun business was and feared that there might be some procedural barrier that would prevent me from dipping my toe into the holy waters for a trial week. I'll never forget Sharon's expression in that moment, her mouth gaping in mid-gum chew, framed fetchingly by her once-blonde hair, now perfectly silver, tiny fragments of which were breaking off and falling gently to her desk like metal shavings. At first I assumed that her speechlessness was caused by sheer admiration. After all, mine was clearly the superior ambition. Given the White King debacle, her desire to learn more about hair-care was certainly well motivated, but how could it compare with buying yourself a first-class ticket on the Jesus Express?

Yet instead of singing my praises, she guffawed and turned to the desks behind us. 'Get this,' she stage-whispered, 'Monica wants to do work experience *as a nun*!' The E's through H's delivered a stinging chorus of scorn, raining down blasphemous 'Oh My Gods!' and sneering at me as if I'd just announced my plan to join some crazy religious cult that regularly harboured serial paedophiles and was run by a super-rich, charismatic leader in a distant tax haven.

Like one of the martyrs of old, I bore their taunts without complaint. *Never mind them*, I thought to myself. *I'll be the one laughing when I'm kicking back in Paradise with my new best friend Jesus, while you E's to H's are stuck in limbo for a few millennia.* (It seemed ungodly for one who aspired to holy orders to wish anyone eternal damnation, so a brief purgatorial stretch was the worst curse I could conjure.)

Still, after that unpleasant experience I kept my nunnish ambitions to myself, assuming that I was alone in my desire for the be-wimpled life. It was only years later that I realised how mistaken I was. In talking to other former Catholic schoolgirls of my generation, I have discovered that a huge number of them harboured the very same desire at one time or another. Of course, there are always exceptions, like White King Sharon, but my friend Kathleen put them in context. 'All the dumb girls wanted to be beauticians, or hairdressers,' Kathleen explained. 'It was the smart girls who wanted to be nuns.'

It's easy to understand why nunning had been popular in medieval times, for it is a thoroughly medieval institution. But what possible attraction could it have had for a healthy, well-adjusted 20th-century teenager? Cynics might put it down to simple brainwashing, and it's true there was no shortage of old-fashioned mind-control practised by Catholic educators at the time. But I don't believe it's as simple as that. While I did have Jesus and Mary relentlessly hammered into my impressionable little brain, I honestly feel that the nun thing was an idea that I cooked up largely by myself.

Once upon a time, nuns were publicly celebrated for their self-sacrifice and lionised for their Good Works, but this had already become a rarity by the time I reached adolescence. In popular culture, they were more likely to be parodied than praised. We now tend to think of nuns as funny, and in a sense they *are* funny, in that they willingly make themselves antithetical to everything that the modern world values. Hey, girls, here's a chance to de-sex yourself, work for free, get up ridiculously early each and every day, and wear sensible shoes for the rest of your life! Who wouldn't jump at that offer?

The more I've thought about this, the weirder it seems. Why did the nun racket still appeal to so many of us, even in the debauched, materialistic, Madonna-saturated 1980s? Stranger still, why were all the cleverest girls attracted to something that seems like such a thoroughly crappy deal? What were we all thinking?

I've occasionally read dedications in books written by successful, convent-educated women and been surprised to find them declaring their deep gratitude to the nuns who taught them. These wonderful and devoted sisters apparently inspired the authors to follow their dreams, strive for excellence, and to be all that they could be.

I wrestle with such sentiments, because the nuns who taught me were not so much inspirational as violent, cruel or flat-out weird. Even looking back now, through more sympathetic, adult eyes, the best I could say is that most of them were sad, or angry, or both.

Only much later did it occur to me that the mismatch between my own experiences and those of these highly successful Catholic author women might have had something to do with the sort of school I attended. Sure, my school, like theirs, was Catholic. But it was what my mother optimistically called a 'regional school', known by everyone else as a 'rundown dump'. Low fees, low standards, and subpar nuns.

Even as a child I knew that envy was a sin, yet still I coveted the luxuries afforded by the fancier Catholic schools. I longed to attend an institution equipped with ponies, regulation hair ribbons and smart, pressed uniforms that everyone wore below their knees. What I didn't understand at the time was that I might also have encountered a better class of nun there. The type who I might later gushingly thank when I'd become world-conqueringly successful and had published an inspiring account of my entirely fabulous, and thoroughly secular, life.

Still, when I look back on the nuns of my own childhood there are a few who stand out from the pack.

There was the young Sister Therese, who at least managed to scandalise the parents by wearing a miniskirt to the school sports carnival. Therese seemed far too racy to be doing God's work, and the general sentiment among the grown-ups was that if she wanted to be young and good-looking she should have chosen another profession. Eventually she did just that. The rumour was that she renounced her vows in order to run off with Father Anthony, a priest who everybody thought was 'lovely', even though he too was young, good-looking and, apparently, using the nunnery as a dating service.

On the other end of the spectrum was the dour Sister Maria. She was Irish, but her eyes consistently failed to smile, and she certainly never dallied inappropriately with any priests. Yet she did have one thing in common with Sister Therese, in that I remember her not for her piety, her dedication to Jesus, or even her charmingly 19th-century morality, but for her questionable fashion choices.

In a way, you can blame the Vatican II reforms for both women's problems. For in freeing nuns from the tyranny of the habit, the Pope was also setting them up for sartorial disaster. In Sister Maria's case, this manifested in a series of adventurously colourful shirts, which made it look as if the pattern fairy had vomited on her bosom.

There were, of course, some nuns who bitterly resisted any such modernising, and the least modern of them all was Sister Josephine. I know that Josephine also managed to leave an impression on many of her other students, although I hope that most of those 'impressions' eventually healed. She was my primary school's singing teacher, but she didn't so much teach as terrorise. Her persistently foul mood, coupled with the onset of dementia, left her wandering the convent hallways, 'disciplining' children left and right, then frequently forgetting that she had disciplined them and whacking them all over again for doing the very thing that she'd set them as punishment. My friend Michael was once dragged from his chair and slapped about the head by her for a minor misdemeanour, then told to wait outside class. Half an hour later, when the poor boy knocked on the door to ask if he could come back in, Josephine fell on him again, giving him an even fiercer beating for being late.

Suffice to say that when news of Josephine's death reached the school, some years after her retirement, it was greeted with the kind of cheering usually reserved for goals in the soccer World Cup.

Yet of all the nuns I knew, the most memorable, and the only one I regard with real affection, was Sister Loretta, who taught me high school science. Unlike the other distant, disengaged nuns, Loretta attempted to connect with us young folk, mostly by talking about sex. Nuns are meant to be more concerned with Jesus than with carnal pleasures, yet Loretta seemed particularly fascinated by God's naughtier gifts, using the fact that she taught biology as a convenient cover for her digressions. She was the first person to enlighten me about masturbation, although I don't think that was her intention, and she certainly didn't use the word. The revelation came when she gave our class a stern talk about the dangers of being too vigorous while washing ourselves 'down there'. If you were in the shower and started enjoying yourself too much you should stop whatever you were doing immediately, she warned, as Jesus most definitely did not approve.

I'm sure this warning triggered dozens of long, curious showers that evening, and in that respect I can honestly say that Sister Loretta did bring a great deal of pleasure into her students' lives.

During another one of our sex talks, she explained to us that we, as women, were like irons – slow to heat up, but also slow to cool down. A man, by comparison, was a light switch. On-off-on-off. How these two wonders of modern electricity came together in a loving embrace, I never fully understood, but the lesson was clear. We must be very careful not to fondle any light switches, lest we accidentally turn them on before we were ready to do the ironing.

In case we suspected that her views on these matters were purely theoretical, Loretta told us about a passionate interlude that had taken place when she was a novice, involving a priest whose hugs felt more special than any others. As Loretta slowly heated up, this priest's light flicked on, and he decided that a life of celibacy was not for him. He did eventually run off with a nun, although sadly it was not Sister Loretta. She was left alone with only her special showers for comfort.

Youngsters are highly impressionable, so if you were lucky enough to be taught by inspirational nuns, then it's not hard to see how you might have been swayed by their example and wanted to follow in their footsteps. But the example set by my lot was not so much calculated to inspire as designed to have you running in fear. I'm not alone in this. When I asked my friends about exactly why they'd wanted to marry Jesus, none of them mentioned inspirational nuns. In fact, most of them gave answers that were vague and heavily qualified, as if they themselves weren't exactly sure why they'd once thought nunning was a good idea.

Of course, most people nurse a wide range of half-arsed career ambitions when they are young, dreams that are never more than a passing fancy. Brain surgeon, actor and President of the United States were all on my list at one time or another. Indeed, just before I decided that I was going to become a nun, my ambition was to be a Jedi Knight. In Year 6, I enjoyed vivid fantasies of turning up to school with Luke Skywalker at my side, strutting around the yard as my friends gasped in jealousy. Luke would inform my teachers that, yes, it was true, The Force was strong in this one, which was why he was whisking me away to join the Rebel Alliance. This fantasy also involved me giving Luke lots of cuddles that made me feel all dizzy between my thighs, but that was only part of the appeal. The scenario was attractive mostly because I wanted to be a superhero, at a time when there were precious few models of hero-dom available to young girls.

By the time I started high school, becoming a nun seemed like a more achievable version of my Star Wars fantasy. And, in many ways, the switch from Jedi to Jesus required relatively little adjustment. After all, *Star Wars* reads very much as a metaphor for Catholicism. Consider Darth Vader who, even after all that he's done, blowing up Alderaan and all that, is still deemed capable of redemption simply on the basis of his deathbed repentance. Which is so Catholic it's ridiculous.

As for nuns, they exert mystery, otherworldliness and spirituality, just like Jedi Knights. They too call upon a powerful, invisible, omnipresent Force and have a penchant for loose, robe-like garments. And, just like Luke Skywalker, a nun's primary aim is to defeat the powers of darkness, while not having intercourse with the only member of the opposite sex in the building.

Of course, the greatest Catholic heroes are those who suffer abysmally for Jesus. To me, as a child, the perfect example of this ideal was Saint Bernadette, the girl who kick-started pilgrimages to Lourdes in France, a sort of Disneyland for the holy. Her story was brought to life by Hollywood in *The Song of Bernadette*, a cheesy old-school biopic that included numerous soft-focus visions of the Virgin Mary, replete with angelic soundtrack and a glowing aura, a bit like Glinda the Good Witch in *The Wizard of Oz*.

The Song of Bernadette won an Academy Award, but the real-life Bernadette was also a big success story, in that she died a horrible, agonising death with tuberculosis in her bones, yet accepted it with grace and charm. Indeed, in the film version, Bernadette hides her painful affliction as long as she can, because Catholics must not only suffer, but suffer in silence. Now that's a role model for a twelve-year-old girl if ever there was one.

None of this seemed sick and twisted to me at the time, because I'd been raised on a steady diet of stories about people whose greatest achievement in life was being killed gruesomely for Christ. While reading my illustrated *Saints of the World* book, I would comfort myself in the knowledge that, while martyrdom did sound unpleasant, the saints in the pictures always managed to keep both their composure and their youthful bloom, even as their eyes were being gouged out, or their flesh crisped at the stake. And why not? They were about to enter the Kingdom of Heaven, which made all the suffering worthwhile. A little like that wave of relief that comes over you as your plane starts descending at the end of a long-haul economy flight to Paris. Sure, after twenty-four hours the cramped conditions and smell of your fellow passengers' farts are almost unbearable, but the knowledge that you'll soon be gorging on croissants in Le Marais serves to dull the pain considerably.

However, at the time it was hard to find anyone who was actually dying for Jesus, at least in suburban Sydney. Given that martyrdom didn't seem to be an option, I figured that my best chance of Catholic heroism would instead lie in a lifetime of piety, humility and single-minded devotion; all things that were synonymous with nun-dom.

For high-achieving girls such as myself, this ideal of extreme self-denial and sacrifice offered a blueprint for a kind of perfection, albeit one with lashings of metaphorical lashings. Forget ridiculous aspirations towards joining the UN or Médecins Sans Frontières. Jesus had already saved the world, so continuing His work was the perfect way for an impressionable girl to get in on the world-saving act.

I don't know many contemporary Catholic schoolgirls, but I suspect that in the 21st century, very few twelve-year-olds aspire to be nuns, even briefly. Certainly, the world has changed a lot since the 1980s, but the real turn-off is the fact that the nun business has changed, and now so much of the drama and theatre that once marked the holiest of professions has been lost. Once again, it was the liberalising influence of Vatican II that did it, forcing nuns to be less extreme and less weird, but also a whole lot less heroic.

Today I'm rather ambivalent about the Catholic Church. Well, ambivalent is probably not a strong enough word. Fury might better describe my current state of mind. Yet, oddly, I do experience a twinge of sadness about the fact that nuns are going extinct – at least in the developed world. Perhaps it's just nostalgia for my youthful idealism, or maybe it's because convents were, in some respects, oddly feminist spaces, where women mixed and mingled with other women while avoiding the ever-present gaze of the patriarchy. But I think the real, deeper reason is that my childhood was happy partly because, and not in spite of, Jesus. Jesus and his gang provided a fairy story that gave many layers of focus, meaning and warmth to my youthful existence. By the time I hit my teens, all that make-believe began to unravel and soon became suffocating. But before that fall from grace, Catholicism was the glue that bound my family and my life together, and nuns, flawed as they were, played a big part in that.

Wherever my nostalgia might come from, it is just a distant twinge. By the time I finally reached Year 10 and got my chance to do work experience, I had long since given up on the nun idea. Instead I wanted to be an actor. So I spent a working week sitting in on rehearsals for an all-female musical being produced at the Sydney Theatre Company. For those five days I got to watch a group of women dressed up in exotic costumes, singing songs and repeating their well-rehearsed lines, over and over again. In a way, it was a bit like the nun business, except nobody got TB and at the end of the day they could all go home and take a nice, long, guilt-free shower.

LEE LIN CHIN & CHRIS LEBEN

The Tweets of Lee Lin Chin

(as told to *The Feed*'s Chris Leben)

‘There's no point in acting your age. If I did I wouldn't be at the pub right now with two 25-year-old models.’

4:50 PM - 2 May 2015

I'm going to the Logies for the first time tonight, which one of the @HomeandAwayTV boys is most likely to put out?

9:39 PM - 9 Jun 2015

If we ever meet, you will remember it for the rest of your life. I will forget the moment you exit my gaze.

5:36 PM - 1 Jun 2015

Sometimes the thug life chooses you, sometimes you choose the thug life. Either way you'll never be a thug like me.

7:23 PM - 16 Dec 2014

There's no point in acting your age. If I did I wouldn't be at the pub right now with two 25-year-old models.

12:08 AM - 3 May 2015

For those asking, I'm not nominated tonight. I don't read the news for awards, I do it for the money, fame & babes #tvweeklogie

12:15 AM - 17 Apr 2015

If you say 'Lee Lin Chin' in the mirror three times I'll come and drink with you.

3:24 AM - 22 Jan 2015

I'm not vain, the song is about me.

9:17 PM - 19 Mar 2015

I'm the voice of a generation, it's just a shame that generation hasn't been born yet.

10:42 PM - 10 Mar 2015

'Hey Lee Lin what are you doing tonight?' 'Your Mum!' #burn

9:24 PM - 7 Mar 2015

Thank god #MardiGras is over. It's the only time of year anyone comes close to competing with my wardrobe.

5:59 PM - 12 Feb 2015

#ValentinesDayAdvice you don't need anyone, you're amazing & no one can compete. Drink a beer in the park by yourself & judge everyone else.

11:30 PM - 29 Dec 2014

Stop calling me your 'spirit animal'! I don't believe in spirituality and animals are for eating. I will NOT be your God food!

3:01 AM - 10 Jan 2015

Who hasn't had gay thoughts?

2:52 PM - 14 Feb 2015

Let's face facts, TV presenters and newsreaders are just people who wanted to be famous but couldn't act or sing.

3:27 AM - 9 Feb 2015

Art is essentially masturbation, ultimately useless and selfish.

11:44 PM - 31 Dec 2014

Your baby isn't special, it's just a poop machine that's a drain on our resources.

6:14 PM - 22 Nov 2014

'Why don't you love me?' – every man who's ever spoken to me.

12:46 AM - 14 Sep 2015

First leaks, now spills? Someone needs to teach this government how to drink #LeeLinforPM #libspill #auspoll #primechinister

2:47 PM - 5 Apr 2015

People seem to think that I'm some mythical comedy unicorn. They are correct.

ANDREW HANSEN

Termination Hotel

❝It had happened so fast, the images were all jumbled in his brain. He thought he'd seen two flaming eyes staring into his soul, like a furious Julie Bishop, but surely that was impossible.❞

I wrote this pisstake of English horror writer Robert Aickman to perform at Ghost Stories, *a monthly show at Sydney's Giant Dwarf theatre. I'm afraid this print version doesn't include eerie lighting, fog, or a spooky soundtrack, so I recommend setting those up in your home or office while you read.*

The office manager was to blame. The office manager, who kept a pet tortoise. Morris had thought this odd, especially when she'd explained that it was not so much a pet tortoise as a personal guard.

The tortoise-cradling lady had stood in the driveway to make certain that Morris set off by her strange short cut that, she pointed out, would save him three blocks of Sydney traffic* and was therefore equivalent to two-and-a-half hours' driving time.

The best that could be said about this short cut was that Morris was now 100 per cent lost in one of those immense new suburbs with quasi-poetic names, like Liberty Lakes or Golden Showers. Or Nugget Swallows.

---

* Sorry about the local reference, but this story was performed in Sydney. For readers not living in Sydney, simply replace 'Sydney' with the name of your home town, and 'traffic' with 'traffic'.

Driving along at sixty kilometres an hour, Morris looked at his watch. No mean feat for a man who kept his watch inside his shoe.

He *had* been driving for hours. He should be almost home by now, but instead he was running out of petrol and rapidly running out of patience with the car radio, which was telling him about their 'no-repeat workday' – an ironic promise given how often it was repeated. The dashboard light, like reruns of *Two and a Half Men*, seemed even feebler than he remembered.

It was dark. Out-of-date street lamps lined identical roads that snaked among towering trees and gates as broad and yellow as Gary Busey's teeth. One suspected the road planners had deliberately avoided straightness, as in the selection of an Olympic swim team.

Morris reached a bifurcation, which left him wondering not only which way to go but also what a bifurcation was. Should he furc left or right? *Furc this*, he thought, and got out of the car.

He couldn't see the moon or stars.

Then he looked up, and could.

It was silent – the houses were set too far back from the road for him to hear the blare of any televisions, which was a blessing, as it was about time for *Bogan Hunters* on 7mate. There were no pedestrians, no traffic, no sound of traffic, no sign of life at all. He couldn't have driven as far as Hornsby, surely?*

Troubled by the quiet, Morris proceeded a short way on foot. Finding that tricky, he switched to both feet. The manager's short cut had sounded promising at the time, but then, lots of people had bought LaserDisc players too.

The left side of the road was lined with weedy vegetation, and the

---

* Again, for those not in Sydney simply replace 'Hornsby' with any other dull but harmless suburb.

right side with buff vegetation that obviously worked out at the gym. *That buff vegetation is smokin'!* thought Morris.

Beyond the vegetation sat a row of hedges – some owners had trimmed their hedges, some hadn't, while still others had given their hedges complete Brazilians.

Walking further along the road would be useless, though the air was warm and fragrant – largely the result of Morris having eaten five Mad Mex tacos for lunch.*

Without warning, something leaped at him from the hedge on his left. He must have royally pissed off a feral cat. The first warning he received was its claws, or perhaps teeth, plunging into his left nipple. He knew his mesh tank top had been a bad idea.

'Owwwwwarrr! Awww-haww-haww-haww-haww! Aaaaarrrghhh, a-haaaaaarggghhhhh!' he said.

Wildly, Morris batted the cat off – that is to say, he hit the cat away, not that he batted it off. This was followed by a sudden silence. He must have hurled the cat a great distance, because there was no trace of the foul beast. It had happened so fast, the images were all jumbled in his brain. He thought he'd seen two flaming eyes staring into his soul, like a furious Julie Bishop, but surely that was impossible. Odder still, he felt it might not have been a cat at all, but … it couldn't be … a feral tortoise?!

There was no reason a pet tortoise couldn't go feral in the same way a cat did, Morris reasoned. Could he have been savaged by a crazed, leaping tortoise?

Morris faltered. His chewed nipple hurt like mad. He couldn't bring himself to touch it, and he was usually quite fond of fiddling with his nips.

---

* Are Mad Mex tacos a local reference? Quite possibly. If you haven't heard of them, just swap in your local mid-quality Mexican chain. Happy José's etc.

He staggered back into the car and set off uncertainly down the road he'd just walked. A terrible thought struck him. What if the tortoise was venomous? It was not greatly enjoyable to imagine the kind of attenuated death that might result from undiluted tortoise venom.

He switched the radio to AM. The road straightened a little, and the number of driveways diminished – though the trees, like the presenters on 2GB, remained dense.* Street lamps were fewer, too, but Morris saw that one of them bore a hanging sign of some sort. It wasn't likely to show a practical destination, but Morris stopped to examine it because, like Steve Price on the radio, he urgently needed a clue.†

The sign was shaped like a sign, and read:

'TERMINATION HOTEL. GREAT MEALS. GOOD SERVICE. OKAY ACCOMMODATION'.

Morris made a decision. He was hungry, lost, nearly without petrol, and had what he still suspected were toxic tortoise tooth marks on his tit. He would ask for dinner and, if he could phone home, maybe stay the night – though he had neither pyjamas nor razor nor Pillow Pet. Morris drove through the massive iron gate, the kind of gate he imagined would front an industrial farm, or Bob Katter's brain.

The ugly driveway was riddled with potholes, as if heavy trucks came in often, or perhaps professional pothole diggers. Morris' headlights swayed and bounced – not because of the potholes, they were just very cheap headlights.

Suddenly, there on Morris' left, he saw it: his left shoulder. He also saw, beyond the shoulder, the Termination Hotel. Thanks to a large

---

*   Oh god, another local. My sincerest apologies. Replace 2GB with your local all-white, all-male, hate-filled talkback station.

†   Steve Price is a talkback radio host on 2GB. Just replace him with any radio personality you especially dislike. Yes, this is another local reference. At this rate I should have just asked you to write the story yourself.

floodlight mounted on the building, Morris spotted a large floodlight mounted on the building.

Was this place really a hotel? Maybe a club of some kind? Surely it was too modern to be one of those B&Bs that looks romantic at first but turns out to be a cramped, badly decorated doll's house that you're forced to share with three awkward couples and the quirky retiree owners whose dream was to open a cute guesthouse but because they've never done two minutes of hospitality training and have a genetic aversion to taste it's like being imprisoned in one of Barbie's cheese nightmares.

Whatever the story, he was going to find out. Morris locked the car. Bit of a mistake, as he forgot to get out first. Ah, he always did this. He unlocked the car, got out, locked it again. Realised he'd left the headlights on. Unlocked it, turned off the headlights, locked it. Damn, he was inside the car again. He unlocked it, got out, got back in, got out again, stood there for a bit, got back in, locked it, unlocked it, got back out, realised he'd lost the key. Got back in, found the key, locked it, turned on the headlights, climbed out the window, reached back in, turned off the headlights, unlocked it, got in, got out, locked it. Suffice it to say the tortoise venom was making Morris a tad vague.

Morris pushed at the door of the house. It was a chunky old door that, like the girls he'd dated in high school, did not open.

He saw a doorbell. He was reluctant to ring, but he rang. The doorbell shouted 'doorbell'. Morris wondered if he was beginning to hallucinate.

He didn't much enjoy standing alone in an odd place under a bright floodlight not knowing what would happen next. Some people probably love doing that, but not Morris.

Fortunately, the door was soon opened by a young, athletic man with blond curls and a blond face. He wore a blond jacket, and smiled blondly.

'Dinner, sir, yes. I'm afraid we've just started, but I'm sure we can accommodate.'

Before Morris had a chance to speak, the blond man had turned and was blondly ushering him along a corridor. On entering the dining room, it struck Morris as slightly too hot. Much too hot. In fact, it was almost as hot as having a sauna in Cairo with Ryan Gosling, which Morris had done once but nobody believed him. The apparently windowless room was lined with thick wall hangings, and the ceiling had been lowered as if to make things easier for any visiting electrician who'd forgotten his ladder and happened to be a dwarf.

Perhaps the room had been designed to dampen the noise, yet the diners were exceedingly quiet. They were crammed together at a single long table running down the centre of the room. *God, do I have to sit with them?* Morris thought. *This is like one of those awful hipster share-plate restaurants.*

But he didn't. There was a separate table along the wall, and the blond lad seated Morris blondly at it. It was a huge table, but only set for one person. *Which must be how Gina Rinehart eats dinner every night ...* thought Morris, unkindly.

Morris looked at the other diners and noticed a very peculiar thing. Underneath the long table, a metal bar ran its entire length. One elderly guest was attached to this bar by a thick chain wound around his calf.

The old man spoke to Morris, pointing at the bloody wound around Morris' nipple. 'I see our little hunter found you.' At this, Morris saw that the old man and all the other diners were each nursing a little bundle – their very own pet tortoises. Each diner was allowing their little tortoise to eat morsels from its owner's plate. The tiny grey heads appeared ravenous as their wrinkled mouths chewed at the raw-looking meat.

From somewhere upstairs, Morris heard a muffled scream. His vision swam and he fell from his chair.

As he lay there, paralysed, he could just make out a woman standing over him. 'It was the venom that guided you here,' she said. It was Morris' office manager, the lady who kept a pet tortoise and had recommended this godforsaken short cut. 'And if there's one thing we promise our pets here at Termination Hotel, it's okay accommodation, good service ... and great meals.'

As one, the hungry tortoises leaped.

SAMI SHAH

I, Pervert

❝Overnight, Pamela Anderson and her cohorts jiggled and bounced their way into our lives. Parents suddenly had to vigilantly guard children from the television, and children had to guard against their parents catching them watching said television.❞

I've always had a strange relationship with porn. I talk about porn in my stand-up, but then you'd be hard-pressed to find a comedian who doesn't. When I first started writing jokes about porn and masturbation, I genuinely thought I was breaking new ground – a perverted Neil Armstrong sticking his penis into the moonscape of Pakistan's collective unconscious. It was only after moving to Australia and meeting other comedians in open-mics and comedy clubs that I realised how ubiquitous the topic of porn is. Male comedians, at least, rarely consider their set complete without a healthy ten-minute chunk on masturbation. But, in my solitary experience as a stand-up comic in Pakistan, I was convinced that I was challenging the status quo in some way.

I received an email from an Australian once that showed me how strangely the rest of the world perceives Pakistani attitudes towards sex. This was around that time when I had been invited to attend the comedy festival on Sydney Harbour. Until the Australian embassy decided the national security of their nation could not be risked by allowing a skinny Pakistani comedian entry, a poster with my name and email address had been plastered all over the festival website. Most of the emails I received were fairly sweet and innocuous – sincerely surprised Australians writing to tell me they didn't realise there was stand-up comedy in Pakistan, which is a reasonable reaction.

Then I got one from a woman that convinced me people outside Pakistan have no idea about the country. The writer had followed a link to a YouTube clip of me performing some of my searingly innovative porn-based comedy in a Lahore college auditorium. She wrote: 'I didn't realise Pakistanis had sex.'

First, let me dispel any further confusion: Pakistanis do, indeed, have sex. We do not rely on some black market cloning technology for reproduction purposes, nor do we spawn from magical pools of amniotic goo, like the Orcs in *The Lord of the Rings*. Indeed, some Pakistanis have quite a bit of sex. Others not as much as they would like to. The men have sex with women; the women have sex with men (although I doubt their experience is anywhere near as satisfying). Sometimes the men even have sex with other men, although discussing or acknowledging that probability is actively discouraged.

In rare cases (but not rare enough), they have happily stuck it in animals as well. Some years ago, the national newspapers reported that a man had been discovered in the act of lovemaking with a donkey. Unfortunately, the donkey belonged to his neighbour. Because this took place in a village, a tribal council was quickly convened, and both the man and the donkey were judged guilty of dishonouring themselves. The donkey was, in keeping with rural customs, killed; the man escaped. I wish I was making some of this up – I remember being quite depressed about the poor donkey's tragic death, although not as depressed as the man must have been.

Social and governmental prohibitions have tried desperately to limit and control all discussion of sex. Pakistan has an extremely Victorian sensibility about the carnal acts: while we are aware that people regularly get naked and push their genitals against each other, we don't think it's something that we need to be reminded of. Much like nose-picking, sex should be done in private – preferably at home, with no one watching. And never in the car.

All attempts at censorship are a futile enterprise, though. Lust, particularly male lust, runs to depths that can never be plumbed. Women may think they have an idea of how deep it goes, but they don't. Even we men don't. Our hunger for sex goes so deep, it frightens even us – past where even the light can reach, below basic lechery and urges, below even the fetishes and standard deviations, it is at such a depth that the pressures crush all comprehension and coherent thought. That is where monsters dwell. Horny creatures that can never be catalogued or understood. Frightful denizens of our lusty ocean floor. And so, even in the most constricting of societies, sex finds a way.

All the way up to the late 1980s, sex was cut out of every Hollywood movie before the Pakistani public could be trusted to view it. Not even a kiss made it through the censors. The hero and heroine would lean towards each other, lips parting and eyes closing ... then suddenly they were enjoying a post-coital cigarette. What happened in between was a mystery. However, extreme violence was left uncensored. We were believed to be more capable of dealing with a heart being pulled out of a man's chest than lips brushing. That is why we Pakistanis are quick to violence and slow to love.

While I was growing up, there were barely two TV channels to watch. One was the state-run channel, PTV, which was fanatically regulated. During the dictatorship of Zia-ul-Haq, a woman couldn't appear on screen unless her head was covered with a modesty-exuding shawl. Even in dramas that included scenes of women waking up from sleep, the characters apparently went to bed with scarves firmly fastened around their heads.

Then, during Benazir Bhutto's prime ministership, the shawls loosened and moved further back on the head, puffs of hair emerging from underneath. When the more conservative government of Nawaz Sharif followed shortly afterwards, the shawls crawled back up to their original places. It got so that you could tell who was in power by the way the PTV female newscasters wore their hijabs.

The other channel at this time only broadcast in the evenings, but, when it debuted in 1990, it was seen as a revolution in TV programming. The entertainment-deprived children of Pakistan got to watch a half-hour of cartoons uninterrupted. Every day brought us the adventures of anthropomorphic warrior cats or space-faring cowboys, followed by ancient British comedies and topped off with an hour of the most notorious failures in US drama history.

But we were not ungrateful. To us, shows like *Manimal* (a man who fought crime by changing into either a panther or a falcon), *The Wizard* (a midget who built toys that always matched his adventurous needs perfectly) and *Street Hawk* (like *Airwolf*, except with a motorcycle) were the greatest things we had ever seen. We spent hours discussing the practical logistics of how Manimal could change into an elephant if need be; to this day, if you see any motorcyclist driving too fast in Pakistan, people refer to him as a 'Street Hawk'.

Years later, when the internet informed me that these shows were actually considered failures in America, I felt betrayed. While American children were watching better shows with better stories and better heroes, we had been tossed the damaged and expired stuff. Much of the breakdown in Pakistani and American diplomacy can be traced to this unhealed wound in our collective psyche.

Then satellite dishes erupted in our sociocultural landscape. Within a few months, every household I knew had installed a large fibreglass bowl with an antenna sticking out the middle. All of a sudden television had become the centrepiece of a cultural revolution. CNN and BBC broadcast 24-hour news that gave us the outside world's perspective on Pakistan; music channels taught us pop, rap, rock and R'n'B; and Indian channels showed us that the enemy was just like us (in that they also watched terrible soap operas about the endless wars between mother- and daughter-in-laws).

And then there was *Baywatch*.

Given what I have just said about the depths of our collective sexual frustration, the effect of those swimsuit-clad buxom bombshells shouldn't come as a surprise. Overnight, Pamela Anderson and her cohorts jiggled and bounced their way into our lives. Parents suddenly had to vigilantly guard children from the television, and children had to guard against their parents catching them watching said television. Moral authorities were up in arms and, if the shrill panic in every social moderator's voice was to be believed, we were on the brink of societal collapse, brought about by slow-motion jogging. The impact on us teenagers – struggling to stay focused on impending examinations – was catastrophic. We couldn't have been more distracted if we had been told to solve differential equations in a strip club. In unison, Pakistani boys tossed aside their textbooks and grabbed their penises.

For me, Pamela Anderson's arrival was almost perfectly timed to coincide with the discovery of masturbation. It was all my friends and I talked about; endless discussions conducted in hushed tones during school lunchbreaks, as we reverentially shared fabricated wisdom with each other. We were in the throes of puberty, and all around us girls were sprouting breasts.

Unfortunately for the boys, we countered those wondrous mutations with itchy underarms and painfully constant erections.

For us it was torture; for the girls, as far as we could tell, it was highly amusing. And so every day, during lunchbreak, we would form a protective huddle and talk about the single greatest shared achievement in our lives.

'I read in my dad's medical books that every time you masturbate you lose a pint of blood,' expounded one boy. His father was a doctor, and so he was our resident authority on all medical matters. 'That means if you masturbate more than twice a day, you could die.'

'Fuck,' said another with a look of horror on his face, 'I masturbated four times last night.'

'You should have orange juice quickly,' offered the medical expert.

'You know, if you masturbate more than a hundred times in your life, you get AIDS,' announced another prodigy. This was followed by a long moment of silence as each boy did some panicked maths.

Finally, I worked up the nerve to ask, 'What's AIDS?'

'Oh, it's a disease that makes you gay. And everyone you touch becomes gay as well.'

'Shit,' said another. 'I think my cousin has AIDS then. He plays with dolls.'

'Don't touch him,' we advised.

And so on. Each day brought some new bit of information about how masturbation could kill you, and each night we all worked hard at separating fact from myth. By the end of seventh grade, had the stories been true, my school would have been struck by an epidemic that attacked only boys, leaving them emaciated husks who played with dolls, had fur on their palms and whose penises had been worn down to tiny, withered nubs.

Back then we had no easy access to pornography. This was still a pre-internet world, in which porn was hard to acquire and hoarded jealously when gained. For two years after I turned eleven, I owned one single porn film: a VHS I had received from a friend whose house was not porn-safe, due to a father who didn't respect the privacy of his pubescent son. I watched that tape over and over, night after night. By the time I was thirteen, I knew every grunt and squeal by heart.

When I found myself growing bored with the single VHS porno I possessed, I asked friends for more, but no one was ready to surrender theirs. So I drew some.

I've always enjoyed drawing. Having discovered comic books years before, I had filled many sketchbooks with detailed renderings of muscular heroes eye-blasting alien menaces while scantily clad women pranced around them. As I grew more and more desperate for something new to inspire my masturbation, I realised that the scantily clad women were a great deal more fun to draw than the muscular hero or his enemy. Except, that is, for when I drew the muscular hero and the scantily clad woman having sex.

I filled page after page with carnal battles. I would draw late into the night, studiously mastering the rules of anatomy and musculature for my own deviant purposes. Within a few weeks I had several-hundred pages filled with graphite copulations; thick sketchbooks crammed inside my cupboard drawers under a camouflage of socks and underwear. And if I had left them there, everything would have been alright.

I'll admit to pride. There was definitely some of that involved in my decision to take those drawings to school and show them off to my friends. I thought they were really damned good works of art. The shading and tonal values in some of them were beyond anything I had done up to that point.

But there was also genuine altruism involved. I actually thought I had come up with a solution to our porn deficit. If someone comes up with a viable alternative to fossil fuel, would that person not want to share their discovery with the world? I simply wanted to provide much-needed relief from the pornographic famine. So I stuffed the drawings into my schoolbag and took them with me ... on the same day that the teachers announced a random bag check.

They hadn't been tipped off. It's not like someone had warned them about a teenage boy smuggling contraband smut into the classroom. No, it was just bad luck on my part. Terrible luck, really. Someone had stolen someone else's brand-new pocket calculator; the victim had complained to the principal; the principal had asked the teacher to announce a surprise bag check.

Three teachers walked into our classroom and asked us all to put our bags up on the desk. Then they went to each bag, took every book out, held the bag upside down and shook it. When they got to my bag, pages and pages of drawings depicting sexual acts in explicit detail tumbled out, fluttering to the ground like autumnal leaves.

My mother was called in. We sat together in the principal's office, she glaring at me as he laid the illustrations out on the table.

'What is this?' he asked.

'Michelangelo drew naked people,' I protested.

'Yes, but not doing it,' he replied.

My mother confiscated all my drawing pencils, took all my comic books and told me I wouldn't be allowed to close the door to my room until I was seventy years old. I was suspended from school for a week. At the end of that week, I was expelled.

There are details from this dark episode that still stab at me occasionally. Jagged shards of memory that poke through the haze of time, and fill me with shame and regret. The staring, wide eyes of the girl seated two rows behind me as I was escorted out of the class by an astonished teacher clutching a bundle of pages. I was going to confess my feelings for this classmate that very day – I'd been working up the nerve to do so for months. The plan was to slip her a small note during recess with 'I like you, do you like me?' written on it. That note was lost in the cascade of incriminating pages.

I remember calling up one of my closest friends the day after and his mother answering the phone: 'He's not allowed to talk to you anymore. I don't think anyone should let their children talk to a pervert like you,' she said.

My mother crying as she told my father over the phone what had happened. I remember thinking about suicide. When you're thirteen and you find yourself without friends or even a school, the future seems quite bleak.

I didn't kill myself. Probably didn't even think about it more than once with any degree of seriousness. I don't even think I stopped masturbating for too long. Two months later, I was admitted into another school. I made new friends and collected new comics. It wasn't long before I even trained myself to forget the whole thing had happened.

The only real evidence of trauma showed itself when, a year after starting at the new school, the teachers announced a surprise bag check. Someone's brand-new pocket calculator had been stolen – I suppose there was a massive underground black market for stolen pocket calculators in Karachi in the early 1990s. The contents of my bag that day were nothing more than a few textbooks and probably a *Hardy Boys Casefiles*, but the moment it was my turn to hand the bag over to the teacher, I started shivering and sweating like a Vietnam War veteran suffering flashbacks while watching *Platoon*.

'Are you okay?' the teacher asked as she handed my bag back to me.

'Yes, miss,' I replied, then excused myself to go vomit in the toilet.

Years later, Pakistan was blessed with internet pornography. No longer were our masturbatory needs limited by scarcity of supply. In the early days of dial-up connections, we used to have to sit and stare at a single picture loading slowly on a flickering monitor. Then video clips appeared online, and internet speeds grew, so that the gap between clicking and relieving was minimal. People without internet access in their homes would go to cyber cafes, gasping and sighing in the privacy of small booths fitted with all the necessities: computer, mouse, chair ... and a box of tissues. It was a glorious time. Porn DVDs could be bought in video stores with a nod and a wink.

I once walked into a store near my house intending to buy a new horror movie DVD, and the man behind the counter nodded for me to come closer as he took the money.

'You look,' he said with a salesman's grin, 'like the kind of man who watches porn.'

When I got home I stared at my face in the mirror, trying to see what it was about my features that tipped him off.

But then Pakistan changed again. In 2012, during a fit of religious cleansing, the government declared a ban on all porn sites. It was decided that internet pornography was ruining the 'youth of the nation'. Clearly, no one bothered to ask the 'youth of the nation' their opinion on all this. Soon, dedicated teams of cyber-censors catalogued and then blocked all the online smut. Pakistani males frantically scoured the web, hoping with each new browser refresh that they would be faced with a wall of questionable thumbnails and a gallery of sad people fornicating sadly, only to be met time and time again by the hateful 'THIS SITE IS RESTRICTED'.

The effectiveness of the ban on online porn was enhanced by the hard work and dedication shown by a fifteen-year-old boy who gave the censors a list of over 780,000 websites that he claimed to have personally checked. For a fifteen-year-old to have done so without being reduced to a smouldering husk is, no doubt, some kind of epic feat that defies human physiology. Unfortunately, what he accomplished so proudly at fifteen, he no doubt came to regret deeply when he turned eighteen. History will remember him as one of the greatest villains mankind has ever known, and only in his later years will he truly appreciate the damage that he wrought. Modern man is not equipped to deal with a world in which he has to make do with imagination alone. I tried. It was all in black and white.

Fortunately for me, I moved to Australia a few months after the ban took full effect. Sometimes I wonder if that was one of my motivations to get out of Pakistan. After all, with my personal history, whenever I masturbate to porn, I'm doing it to get revenge on society.

From I, Migrant *by Sami Shah (Allen & Unwin 2014)*

ROZ HAMMOND

Because You're Worth It

———⊰◦◦◦⊱———

❛Her pupils were dinner plates from which she gorged on the rare and exquisite beauty that beamed from the looking glass. This, she decided, is what God must feel like when She looks in the mirror.❜

———⊰◦◦◦⊱———

It began with Pamela Moore's spectacularly successful trip to Paris. Max, her husband of seventeen-and-a-half years, had been speaking at a tile, cork and hardwoods conference at the invitation of one of the larger French parquetry firms. For the past fortnight they had wined and dined atop all the finest floors in Europe, from Scandinavian elm to Belgian yew.

The conference invitation had arrived at a most suitable time, because for some months, Pamela Moore had been obsessing over her own mortality. She had grown profoundly maudlin – at times spending upwards of three hours simply staring into a mirror and naming each of her individual wrinkles.

Max was otherwise occupied. At the peak of his managerial powers, he was increasingly staying out late with various colleagues and coves from his many clubs and committees.

Toby, Pamela's first-born, had grown ambivalent towards her, except for when he wanted to borrow the Audi or invite some friends down to their chateau in Portsea. Toby and his current squeeze, Miranda, a sulky and over-sexed young woman, were ensconced in the beach house at that very moment. Supposedly studying for their practice exams, they were in fact alternating between chopping out lines of cocaine, dropping suspect GHB and having clumsy, frenetic sex in the Moores' king-sized waterbed.

Pamela's sixteen-year-old daughter, Annabelle, whose indifference towards her mother was the stuff of legend, was away until Christmas, pirouetting and pas de deuxing her way through a ballet scholarship in Geneva.

With Max consumed by discussions of lacquers and laminates in the Faubourg Saint-Antoine, Pamela spent long Parisian days in the salons and spas of the 2nd arrondissement. Having decided that the ULTIMATE PROCEDURE be saved until it was time for her to dazzle as the Mother of the Bride sometime in the next decade, Pamela was desperate to find some other method with which to stall the voracious hounds of time.

It was during one of those long afternoons of plucking and pinching, injecting and firming, that the lithe and sleek Monsieur Richot first appeared to her, like some sort of holy vision. Five-foot-nothing, with a tumbling curtain of blue-black hair that seemed on the verge of consuming him whole, Claude Rimbau Richot slid silently into the chintz-covered armchair beside Pamela's oxygen booth.

'You are Mrs Pamela Moore, *oui*?'

Jolted out of her blissful reverie, Pamela was met by the largest pupils she had ever seen; only a tiny trace of pale blue was visible around their border. It looked like he was experiencing a once-in-a-lifetime optical eclipse.

'Dr Langazho has told me of your *petite* problem, Madame. I think it is only I who can help. *Oui*?'

Richot was referring to her recent experiment with the chichiest muscle-paralysing injection on the market, a test that had found her slightly allergic and left her looking like an extra from *Star Wars* for three full days of the last week. The litigation-paranoid Langazho had advised against further treatment, urging her to cast her net wider in her quest for cosmetic perfection.

The face now perched in front of Pamela was line-free and a deep golden brown. Only a heavy jowl betrayed his middle age. A thin layer of perspiration bubbled on his upper lip.

Drawing a tiny vial from beneath his camel-coloured Marchante coat, Monsieur Richot tapped the bottle gently over his palm. A droplet of pure light slipped into his hand, a pea-sized globule of iridescent liquid that seemed to hover above his flesh.

Bewitched by its shimmer, and the €300-worth of oxygen coursing through her blood, Pamela Moore decided she simply must have this magnificent pearl. She turned her face towards Monsieur Richot.

With the aid of a tiny spatula, the Frenchman applied the merest suggestion of the elixir to Pamela's eyelids and gently pressed his palms against her eye sockets. His clammy, trembling hands then proceeded to lightly brush the rest of her face, neck and décolletage with the jewel-like balm.

Pamela's eyes stung, and a searing flash of white light pierced her retinas. Suddenly she was awash with a sense of almost spiritual awakening. Light and buoyant, she felt a million giddy, wonderful thoughts ricochet around her brain, each more perfect and insightful than the last. Then the rush was simply gone, so rapidly she wondered if it had even occurred. However, on turning to the mirror, she beheld such a vision of loveliness that her breath quite left her.

With a tiny bow, Monsieur Richot withdrew to give her some privacy. Once he had closed the salon door behind him, he secreted himself in a nearby supplies cupboard, opened his vintage snuff box and snorted deeply. The surge of euphoria had him salivating over the prospect of selling this batch to the cashed-up clubbers in Majorca.

Meanwhile, Pamela Moore's face blazed as if lit by an internal, million-watt globe. Her pupils were dinner plates from which she gorged on the rare and exquisite beauty that beamed from the looking glass. This, she decided, is what God must feel like when She looks in the mirror.

With a discreet clearing of his throat, Monsieur Richot announced his return to the room. Pamela reluctantly tore her gaze away from the mirror to face him. Smiling crocodile-wide, he clasped her hand quickly, their sweaty palms meeting with a distinctive *thwack*.

'This is amazing, *oui*?'

She squinted, trying to focus on the little Frenchman's eager face. His features were blurred and fuzzy, shrouded in some sort of cloud. Not exactly distorted, but like an image projected through a Vaseline-smeared lens in some old pornographic number. Feeling a surge of affection for the bronzed gnome, she lunged towards him with outstretched arms.

'Surely you will want some more of this miracle?' Richot cooed as he extracted himself from Pamela's overzealous embrace.

She could only nod dumbly, transfixed by the tiny image of herself she had just spied in Richot's obsidian orb.

'This is very exclusive, Madame,' Richot advised. 'It has all sold out except for my personal supply. Just twelve bottles left in the world. There may be more later, but for now this is all. But I think for what you are after, it is perfect, *oui*?'

Monsieur Richot's instructions were crystal clear. Less was definitely more. One vial properly administered should last twelve to eighteen months. 'Just the size of a pea, Madame. It is very powerful, *oui*?'

With focus fixed firmly on her own reflection, Pamela agreed to depart with a sizeable sum in euros. 'Name a price, you glorious little man.' Using the sleek terminal that the monsieur had whipped from his

Marchante, she transferred the equivalent of three months' wages into the Frenchman's Swiss account.

Transaction complete, she floated out into the day, taking the steps down to the street four at a time.

Back in the salon, Richot clapped his hands joyfully. This had been a most unexpected coup. It was his young lover, Jean-Marc, who had accidentally created this wonder drug while cooking up party pills in the bathroom of their Montmartre apartment – their gift for Daniel and Nils' commitment ceremony on the weekend.

After the amateur chemist had snorted a line and knocked back a few glasses of *blanc*, his boisterous twerking had nudged a tray of amphetamine all over the vanity. Jean Marc managed to retrieve it all, except for the portion that had plonked into his open jar of moisturiser. This he simply stirred into the cream, hastily hiding his blunder beneath the jar's lid.

It was only later that evening, when following his anti-ageing regime, that Richot discovered the thrill of his accidental blend.

En route to the airport to catch a flight to Majorca, Richot had delivered a bag of amphetamines to an old school friend, the social drug enthusiast and recently deregistered doctor Langazho. By way of small talk (and an attempt not to appear too eager about the party favours being bestowed upon him), Lanhazho mentioned the middle-aged Australian he had seen the week before, and her reaction to the filler. Such a reaction was rare; both men had received the procedure many times with no ill effects.

It was when Langazho excused himself to attend to another client that Richot had a deliciously wicked idea. What if he presented the batch of amphetamine-loaded, totally useless moisturiser in his carry-on luggage as some kind of beauty miracle? He had nothing to lose and plenty to gain. And he was all too aware of how easily the desperately unhappy were separated from their money.

Desperate Pamela Moore may have been, but now she was far from unhappy.

The fortnight following her return from Paris proved a most agreeable time. Weight fell from her body, dropping her to a suspiciously muscular size four, and the magnificent balm that she was now applying hourly was keeping her skin as firm and silky as the proverbial baby's bottom.

The fact was, Pamela felt better than she had in years, and the occasional disconcerting accidents that marred her otherwise perfect days were dismissed as the consequences of jet-lag – as was her inability to sleep for more than twenty minutes at a time. Her recently acquired penchant for shoplifting she didn't even try to explain. She simply secreted her impressive haul of contraband in a hole in the back garden and covered it with hessian sacks and cardboard.

When Pamela wasn't on a robbery spree or shouting at strangers on railway platforms, she spent many hours lying on the sofa with her lids fluttering halfway between open and closed: an unnatural sight that was often accompanied by murmuring, twitching and giggling. Her children, long accustomed to ignoring her, didn't even notice the difference.

Pamela's blissful fugue ended abruptly in a small interrogation room on the first floor of David Jones. At the behest of the manager, Pamela Moore pulled from her winter coat all manner of glass and reflective objects: a vase, an antique mirror, tawdry silver moon earrings, a pewter mug. The woman staring back from their shiny surfaces was terrified and bewildered.

'But I don't know how they got there. I didn't take them. It wasn't me. Someone must have put them in my pocket.'

Perplexed by this smartly dressed woman, who was obviously higher than their store's prices, the manager summoned the police.

Pamela sat quietly, aside from the loud grinding of her jaw, unable to concentrate on anything except a small paperclip on the floor, which she could have sworn was speaking to her. Her dull-eyed acquiescence lasted right up to the point where a stout female police officer arrived and attempted to remove the contents of her bag.

A furious tussle ensued, climaxing when the remaining seven vials of Monsieur Richot's secret blend smashed on the floor. Pamela sobbed and wailed, clawing at the miracle cure as it drained away like the sands of time. Defeated, she used her last reserves of energy – and a broken vial of elixir – to launch a lacerating attack on the unfortunate PC, opening an artery that gave the bare little room a welcome splash of colour.

'Darling, look what I've found.'

Monsieur Richot gazed out from his sunbed as the heavily bandaged Jean-Marc – recovering from brand-new pec implants, courtesy of one Pamela Moore – came towards him with a moisturiser pot. A thick, potent powder lay at the base of the jar. Licking his finger and dipping it into the pot, Monsieur Richot tested a small sample.

'*Mon dieu*, that's pure. It must have made the moisturiser evaporate.'

'Richot, dear, don't you feel just a teensy bit bad about passing it off as a cosmetic marvel?'

'*Pourquoi*? What I sold was no more expensive or ineffective than any other skin cream. At least Mrs Moore would have had fun finding that out. *Non*?'

LIAM RYAN

Total Product Recall

'It's all part of BluVu's patented
Always There, Always Waiting automatic
assistance programme. '

Congratulations on your purchase of BluVu, the compact domestic support unit that lives to serve. Put your feet up, say goodbye to chores and let this 'must-have robot butler' (*TIME Magazine*) make life a breeze!

We trust that you will not encounter any problems with your BluVu unit, but in case there are teething issues, these Frequently Asked Questions should help you on your way to a hassle-free home.

I can't turn the unit off. Is there a switch I can't see?
No. In order to make life even easier for you, your BluVu unit will simply turn itself off when it is good and ready.

Is there a way to reduce the amount of eye contact the unit engages in?
Not really. The best solution is for you to just get used to it.

Although the waddle is cute, is there a way to adjust my BluVu's stride so it sounds less like I am being followed by a bag full of cutlery?
No.

Why does the product appear to be mapping my every move and watching me sleep?
It's all part of BluVu's patented Always There, Always Waiting automatic

assistance programme. [*See also* **Did the unit just follow me to work?** *and* **Why has the unit memorised my browser history?**]

What is with the blood-curdling scream every time I leave the house?
Just consider this BluVu's way of saying, 'I love you, master. Goodbye.'

I'm noticing subtle changes in my BluVu unit's behaviour. Is there a chance it is hiding my keys in an effort to keep me housebound?
Every model adjusts differently and will try to help you in unique ways.

Why did you give it teeth?
To eviscerate its prey and your enemies.

Though small, my BluVu unit seems capable of super strength. Are its frequent shows of force (lifting furniture, kicking down doors, throwing pot plants/pets over the fence etc.) intended to impress or intimidate me?
Can't it be both?

Why does this thing really have it in for my dog?
BluVu has identified the dog as a 'success inhibitor' and is just trying to help.

Last night, while discussing with my partner how we might put our BluVu unit to S-L-E-E-P, it ceased responding to commands then beat up the microwave. Is it upset?
BluVu has an inbuilt sensitivity capability so that it can best anticipate your needs. So yeah, probably.

My energy bills have gone through the roof. Is there a chance my BluVu unit has tapped into the mains in order to power a secret nerve centre it has set up somewhere inside my house?
That is crazy talk.

My BluVu unit has engineered an exact replica of itself, and now both have set to work on constructing another one. How do I dissuade them from pilfering electrical cables and metal from the house to build more of themselves?

Best not to get in the way. Your BluVu unit(s) are probably just creating an army of assistants to help you crush your problems.

Since date of purchase, why do I keep getting mystery calls from the same number?

I wouldn't know anything about that.

Oh my god, are these calls coming from inside the house?

Most likely.

While investigating a power outage, I found a hive of wire and BluVu units that runs throughout the crawl space and underneath the house. It has since begun to seethe and churn. How do I apply a factory reset?

But we've come so far.

Jesus, our BluVu unit(s) are everywhere. How do I request a technician to come to our house and save us?

A technician can't help you now.

We are holed up in the bathroom while an army of fifty or so BluVus tries to beat the door down – are we doomed?

Unless you can identify the swarm leader and dismantle it, I'd say so.

What will they do to us when they find us?

Make you their king!

Really?

No.

Why on earth would someone create a product capable of such evil?

I have my reasons.

Has a BluVu unit compiled this FAQ?

;)

This is madness.

Is that a question?

Is this madness?

Yes, it is.

I need to find the original unit and convince it to call off the assault. Where will I find it?

It's behind you.

JANE RAWSON

Bob Brown's Farewell Speech

―――⊃∘∘⊂―――

❝Of course, Canberra is gone now, and all of the honourable members and the press gallery with it. I shouldn't speak ill of the dead. Instead, I'll explain why today is a happy day, and not just because we've lost the Murdoch press.❞

―――⊃∘∘⊂―――

The environmentalist and politician Bob Brown gave this farewell speech on the day that a firestorm threatened to overrun the last outpost of humanity, a small settlement in Tasmania's south-east.

A re you okay? Is everyone okay back there? Alright then, let's rest here awhile.

First, I want to thank all of you – my fellow Earthians – for being here with me today. You've come so far, achieved so much, to be here this afternoon. To the survivors of last summer's Victorian holocaust, I salute you. Those who made it here after Sydney was cut off from food supplies, who escaped the slaughter of Surry Hills, I can only imagine the horrors you have seen. And the orphans whose parents sacrificed everything to get them here as Brisbane went under, I'm sorry we couldn't do more for you. All of you have contributed so much to our little community, and I thank you all for your self-sufficiency, your resilience and your undimmed hope.

Well, this isn't how I hoped to say goodbye to you. But the fire is coming – it's just over that hill – and it looks like today we're going to have to do that. Say goodbye. There's so much more I wish we could have done. But in the end – because it does look like the end is here – we still have an awful lot to be grateful for. All our days on this wonderful Earth. We still have some tea, don't we? That Kevin Rudd blend? Yes, thanks, that would be lovely.

I'm sure you all have your own memories that you hold dear: the things we've done, the people we've been. What do they matter, now that the minds they're held in are about to become dust? No one will come after us to read our books, watch our films, water our gardens or wrap themselves in the blankets we've knitted. We have only a few hours left to relive the time we first saw our babies' fingers curl around our own, and then that memory will, along with us, be gone. I can't say I'll miss being told that people like me were too perverted to raise children – but hey, it was something, wasn't it, to have had this life? To have known, seen, felt so much. Trevor Chappell's underarm bowl. Kate and William's wedding. The Big Banana. Camp Gallipoli. Economic rationalism has given us so much.

Still, it hasn't all been defeat. You know how much it meant to me that we got so close to world democracy towards the end there; so close to kicking off that brilliant global career in togetherness. Remember when my colleague in the Senate told me it would never be a goer? Good old Freddie – does anyone know what happened to him in the end? Really? That's horrific! Well, fate works its surprises in both directions, and I certainly take some comfort in that ... Where was I? Oh, yes: 'Do you know how many Chinese there are, Bob?' he said. I knew how many there were. Well, round about. I couldn't have said exactly. But I'm not sure he was questioning my mathematical prowess. I think his point was there were far too many Chinese for his taste. At any rate, I suppose what he was saying was that it just doesn't do to hand votes out willy-nilly. Look at what happened in South Africa: you give everyone the vote and some black bloke ends up running the place. Imagine adopting that globally! One person, one vote – well, we'd be bound to end up represented by a Chinese fellow, wouldn't we? Or, God forbid, an Indian. Better off, he reckoned, letting the multinationals figure it out between themselves. One share, one vote, 'a new birth of freedom ... so that government of the people, by the Board, for their profit, shall not perish from the Earth', as I'm sure Abraham Lincoln would have said had he won a seat in the 2013 federal election.

Well, government of the people has perished, or it soon will. I can hear the fire now. I suppose the wind must have changed. Those embers aren't good news; we'll need to get going soon. I'm sorry to say that it looks like none of us will be here to see whatever the Earth dreams up next. But someone will be here to see it. Not the tigers – the tigers are gone, of course; the tiger quolls, too, though that didn't make quite the same splash. No more penguins or prawns or pied oystercatchers; no oysters to catch, for that matter. But we shouldn't be so selfish as to think the end of us is the end of it all. Optimism, friends! Optimism, fellow Earthians! There are endless species ready to step in where we have failed.

I'd always hoped that once we reached the state of one human, one vote that we'd pause for a moment, congratulate ourselves and then realise that we had come, still, such a little way. What about everyone else? What of all our fellow travellers on this small blue dot?

One creature, one vote: it was my fondest hope. We all have to live here; it seems to me we should all get a say in how the joint is run. I'm sorry I didn't get to campaign on this point. Andrew Bolt would have had a heart attack; I mean, had he survived the Eastern Suburbs Sewage System Explosion. What hilarious columns he would have written: 'Bob "Bonkers" Brown demands ant-sized ballot papers for insect voters'. And I can hear the House of Reps now. How would we tell the difference between the celery-top pine candidates? And how would they even make their way to Parliament House, Bob? You wouldn't want us to have to cut 'em down and chuck 'em on a flatbed would you, Bob? Thank goodness the country was run for so long by such rational, level-headed folk. We can look around us now and revel in the wonderful society they've created. Jemima, I think Oliver's hat is on fire. You might need to stop it spreading to his hair.

Of course, Canberra is gone now, and all of the honourable members and the press gallery with it. I shouldn't speak ill of the dead. Instead, I'll explain why today is a happy day, and not just because we've lost the Murdoch press. It is a hopeful day, the start of a wondrous journey into the enticing centuries ahead. We may be the last outpost of humanity, but we are not the last intelligent life. Humans have done wonderful things; of course we have. I think fondly of *Middlemarch* and Edith Campbell Berry, of New York's Chrysler Building and Launceston's Holyman House, of the songs of Eric Bogle, Paul's buttered scones, hot baths and GORE-TEX boots: I'm not diminishing our magnificent achievements. But on what appears to be our final day it is important we remember that we are really not that special, and that our ordinariness means we are not alone.

Humans have always searched the stars, run our radio receivers over far-distant galaxies in the hope of hearing a blip, a peep, some stoic signal that has travelled hundreds, thousands of light-years to tell us there is someone else out there. Up, up, away – we have always cast our eyes heavenwards. But life is here, fellow Earthians. It is all around us. Intelligent life; loving life. We have longed for someone we could talk with and never stopped for a moment to learn the language of the creatures who surround us.

The dolphins are gone now, the whales too. We had so many opportunities to learn from them, and they from us. We could have joined forces, shared our experience of life on land, discovered the intricacies of life underwater.

We missed those opportunities but, more importantly, the universe has now lost them too. We enslaved the pigs to keep them quiet; we won't see a porcine empire on Earth any time soon. We could have learned, surely, a little from our primate cousins, but instead we sacrificed the bonobo, the chimp, the gorilla for mobile phones and tablet computers. As the wonderful Mr Vonnegut once said, so it goes.

Still, despite the destruction, all is not lost. The cuttlefish, you see, give me hope. The octopuses, ever-evolving, that wily Common Sydney Octopus extending its range and demanding a rebrand as the Common Freycinet Octopus – they give me hope too. And the squid. These cephalopods, with their advanced problem-solving skills, their complex communication and their ability to get used to warmer water and shifting prey. We pride ourselves on our intellectual abilities, but the ocean has clever creatures to rival what we've achieved. The world may lose humanity, but the grand experiment of intelligent life on Earth is not over with our passing; how arrogant of us to ever think it would be.

And intelligence isn't everything. Of course, we value it: it's what sets us apart. But it is just one of the many brilliant strategies for survival that evolution has developed. Cooperation is just as important. Empathy; care for your fellow creatures. Who knows what kinds of minds are yet to come? New species for this new world, the descendants of today's algae, cockroaches, pine beetles, mosquitoes and snakes. Remember, there was a time when the dinosaurs would have scoffed at our ancestors: they'd have looked down on our little ratty forebears the way we dismiss the lives of houseflies and chooks. But look around you – look at the faces of your friends and your family, those beautiful smiles, those treasured hands and eyes – and see how far those little rats have come. If we can be sure of one thing it is that evolution will bring fresh miracles, a joyride of new life.

It's getting hot, isn't it? I think it's time to go. Has everyone had something to drink? Good.

Push on towards the water, friends. Battery Point might make it through – that old sandstone has seen a lot in its time. You might yet live to see tomorrow. But even if you don't, this isn't the end of us. Remember Kevin Gilbert's immortal words, 'Creation flows to me, through me, within me ... the universe is part of me, as I am part of it.' We are not just our species – we are a tiny segment of the whole brilliant experiment of life on Earth, our DNA shared almost entirely with every other living creature. We are tangled up with everything that has been and that ever will be. As long as something lives, we live too.

Go well. Head for Salamanca Place. I'll stay here in case there are stragglers. Hurtling to death, friends, I am alive.

Originally appeared in Seizure *2015*

JAMES COLLEY

The Backburner's Six Most Burnable News Stories of 2015

‘Gillard was unavailable for comment at the time of printing, as any attempt to answer our questions was greeted with uncontrollable laughter and the phrase 'it's on'.’

The Backburner is Australia's premier satirical news source. Written by James Colley and a team of thousands (read: five), The Backburner covers all the stories the other papers won't touch. Mainly because they don't exist.

Reclaim Australia accidentally reclaims 1930s Germany

An attempted bigot convention has gone awry over the weekend as attempts to 'Reclaim Australia' have led to hate groups accidentally reclaiming the fascist rhetoric of the rise of the Third Reich.

The group met with the express purpose of reclaiming an Australia that they believe had once existed because they heard about it in a Slim Dusty song. Unfortunately for organisers, the violent intimidation and overt racism of the event meant that all that was reclaimed was the spirit of fear and hostility of one of the bleakest periods of human history.

'I suppose this was a pretty massive oversight,' said one organiser. 'I guess if we wanted to reclaim Australia then we would have to show up and engage heavily with Indigenous culture, being as they are about as Australian as it gets.

'I mean, there were dudes here with swastika tattoos. Swastikas! I've got tattoos I regret, but surely as that's being inked in you must think, *Well, this is permanent and maybe one day I'd like to have a conversation with a reasonable human ... I'm making a terrible mistake.*

'Maybe we just got the name wrong. Maybe 'Reclaim Australia' was too vague. What we meant to say was that anyone who is different to us is bad. Did that message convey?'

However, organisers were reluctant to admit the event was a complete failure, saying that there were some positives to come from the event.

'We did manage to stave off sharia law for another day. Sure, no one was trying to institute sharia law and this whole thing was just dog-whistling racism, but still, we stopped sharia law. We also stopped the Hindu religion becoming mandatory, an invasion of mammoths and a whole range of other things that had no chance of happening.

'We're basically heroes, if you were to change the definition of "hero" to the opposite of what it is now.'

Anti-racism advocates also admitted there were some positives to be taken from the event, saying that now that we know how to gather all the bigots in one place, all that we need is the technology to summon a comet to a specific location.

Man dehydrates after discovering water is halal certified

A Brisbane man has died of dehydration today after refusing to consume water following the revelation that technically water is halal certified.

42-year-old Brisbane local Keith Sheen, a noted opponent of what he believes 'halal' to mean, brazenly refused to consume water or any drink containing water to protest halal certification. He also vocally expressed his outrage that two-thirds of the planet he inhabited were composed of what he called 'the Muslim liquid'.

His body succumbed to dehydration earlier this morning.

Mr Sheen had previously complained about products in his local supermarket containing dietary information such as halal certification.

'Why should I have to look at that when it doesn't apply to me?' Mr Sheen once wrote to his local newspaper. 'It's the same with these peanut allergy warnings. I don't personally have a peanut allergy so we should get rid of them for everyone. It's only fair.

'You know what harm it does me to look at halal certification? None at all. But what if the answer was "some"? That would be unacceptable.'

Sheen insisted that his objection to halal certification was not on the basis of racism or anti-religious bigotry, claiming he was not personally a racist but just 'said racist things and acted in a racist way all the time'.

A statement released by his family praised Sheen's commitment to his principles. 'Our father was a man of principle, and his death is another sign that sharia law has gone too far, or perhaps not far enough. We are not clear on what sharia law is or how far it should go.'

A memorial service will be held for Keith Sheen this Wednesday. The wake has been delayed due to complications in finding non-halal certified food to serve.

Abbott: Australia won't blindly follow US to equal marriage; it's not like a war

The Australian Government has declared it is not compelled by the Supreme Court ruling on equal marriage and will not blindly follow the United States into social reforms as though they were some kind of war in the Middle East.

While momentum is growing in Australia for equal marriage reforms, the prime minister has warned that we must stop and consider the implications of applying such measures to Australia and not treat such a fundamental decision with the kind of flippancy you would show entering an unending ground war in an already destabilised region.

'This decision could not be more important,' said Prime Minister Abbott. 'We cannot rush into such a thing. We are not merely an extra state of America. We would only blindly follow them if it were for a poorly thought-out military campaign.

'We want to do something because we want to do it. This isn't the case here. Surely, the overwhelming majority of Australians do want us to do this, but that's probably because they saw America do it.

'We're our own people. We don't just do everything that the United States, Ireland, New Zealand, the United Kingdom, Iceland, Canada, Brazil, Argentina, Mexico, France and all the others have done.

'If all those nations jumped off a bridge, and our population really wanted to also jump off a bridge, would we do it? The last thing you should do in a democracy is listen to the will of the people. This isn't a popularity contest – that's just how we get in a position to say this isn't a popularity contest.'

The Prime Minister has admitted that the fight against equal marriage seems to be a lost cause.

'Sure, we might be on the wrong side of history, but sometimes it's important to stand for what you believe in. How am I supposed to look my grandchildren in the eye and tell them that I let two people who loved each other get married under my watch?'

Julia Gillard rushed to hospital after overdosing on schadenfreude

Former Prime Minister Julia Gillard is under observation at Royal Prince Philip Hospital after overdosing on schadenfreude, the pleasure derived from witnessing someone else's misfortune.

Gillard was found in her residence clutching an oversized bag of popcorn and watching the ABC's *7.30*. An ambulance was called to the Gillard residence and she was taken to hospital, where she remains in a stable, non-life-threatening condition. Hospital staff were quick to caution that it was not all good news, however.

'Unfortunately we were unable to wipe the smile off her face,' said a hospital spokesperson. 'We tried everything we could, but it won't budge. This is unusual for a simple case of excessive schadenfreude.

'Whoever is triggering this episode must really, really deserve it.'

Gillard was unavailable for comment at the time of printing, as any attempt to answer our questions was greeted with uncontrollable laughter and the phrase 'it's on'.

A spokesperson for Gillard thanked the medical staff at the Royal Prince Philip Hospital for their dedicated work and insisted that there is no need for concern.

'We appreciate the outpouring of tributes we've received, but there is no need to worry. The only thing around here that's terminal is the Abbott Government.'

Bill Shorten caught in Chinese finger trap

Opposition Leader Bill Shorten has caused a stir by appearing in question time with his hands still stuck in a Chinese finger trap.

'Obviously, this situation isn't ideal,' said Mr Shorten, as he addressed Parliament. 'But what we need to be focusing on is Mr Abbott's failure to produce a fair budget, not whether or not my fingers are currently trapped in a traditional Chinese puzzle.

'The fact is, the honest working families of this country care about whether education will be affordable for their children, not whether the opposition leader has the use of his index fingers.'

Prime Minister Tony Abbott immediately pounced on the blunder as an opportunity to attack Labor, claiming this proved Shorten was unfit for government.

'How can we trust a leader to have his finger on the button, if those fingers are constantly being imprisoned within simple puzzles?'

Abbott has faced accusations of hypocrisy, as it was revealed this statement was made while both his hands were independently stuck in two different pickle jars.

'This is an entirely different situation,' claimed Abbott. 'For starters, this is intentional. I love having my hands in pickle jars. It preserves their youthful vigour. Also, it makes them smell of pickles, which is a constant delight. And it stops me from strangling Malcolm every time he opens his goddamned craw.'

This was the latest in a series of embarrassing incidents for Shorten, who has previously been unable to rise to ask questions due to being entirely covered in honey. However, the Opposition Leader remains adamant that he is fit to lead.

'We shouldn't be focusing on how many times I've locked myself in the office, or that one time I ran out of the chamber because Joe Hockey threw a tennis ball. We need to join together to stop the Abbott Government.

'If we don't, Australia will be locked into a dismal future, like two fingers locked in a hellish tube that seemed so simple when I was given it. Please ... please help me.'

Young white male decides Australia Day isn't problematic

After a long hour of soul-searching, young Australian Timmy McGrath of Willoughby has decided that Australia Day isn't problematic, and at the time of reporting is 'smashing tinnies' with a clear heart.

For a few minutes Timmy respectfully and solemnly dwelt on the complicated history of today's date to the First Australians. He thought about how he would feel if his nation was taken from him and even considered the endemic racism still experienced, particularly on days like today, before ultimately deciding that he would really prefer to enjoy today free of any guilt, complication or critical thought.

'I think everybody just needs to calm down,' he said. 'I mean, how long are you going to stay mad about all those murders that happened to your people? Or the theft of your land by colonisers?

'Sure, I'm still mad about the *Star Wars* prequels, but that's different. That's really important. And fortunately for me, there isn't a day where everyone gets a day off work to really properly celebrate the release of *The Phantom Menace*.'

Timmy indicated that it wasn't that he wasn't sympathetic, but rather that he didn't get many public holidays and wanted to make the most of them.

'It's just that I love this country and want to be able to celebrate it for a day without thinking about how that country was violently constructed on top of hundreds of nations that were already existing.

'Besides, that was ages ago. I never took anyone's land from them,' he said, still standing on the stolen land. 'All I've really done is thoughtlessly benefit from a privileged life.

'I mean, sure, if you thought about how the continued history of racism towards Indigenous people results in a huge disparity in literacy and mortality rates, you would be horrified at the idea of a nation patting itself on the back on today of all days. Fortunately, what I do is not think about that. Have a good time. Listen to the *Hottest 100*. Chill out.'

While he hasn't contacted any Indigenous leaders with his thoughts on everyone 'just kicking back and enjoying the day', Timmy is sure that they'd get behind the idea in a moment.

'You've got to enjoy it while it lasts. I mean, whether it takes five, ten or twenty years, there is no way Australia Day can remain on this date. We may not have many left. Let's party while we can.'

LIAM PIEPER

Catching the Spirit

‘She tells me I'm holding a karmic debt from a past life in which I had great power and used it selfishly; I was a great intellectual or a priest, and, also, 'probably a paedophile'.’

I'm in Nimbin, chasing a story, and I don't like the way the turkey is looking at me.

The second I arrived at the hostel, set on an abandoned farm at the edge of the rainforest, the turkey started stalking me with the slow malevolence of a traffic cop. All day, every time I look at it, it folds out its plumage like a switchblade and runs a feint at me.

The turkey is trying to establish dominance. The turkey does not know how badly it has underestimated me. I'm here in Nimbin covering a story for an important and influential magazine that, truly, I have no business writing for. The commission for the Very Important Magazine will pay more than I usually make in a year and establish me as a proper, grown-up writer. Being here on Magazine business means that I am fit to burst with hubris; this puffed-up, pugilistic turkey could be my spirit animal.

Nimbin is a countercultural enclave in the heart of the northern shires of New South Wales. On the drive in, I passed tiny farms nestled in patches of rainforest, where naked men taking the sun in deckchairs would surprise me, popping up sudden and unlovely as mushrooms after the rain, providing fleeting, peripheral glances of wrinkled gnarly flesh as I sped by. Less than an hour's drive from Byron Bay, where waves of gentrifying sea-changers are slowly turning the coastline into northern

California, things are different out here. As you head further inland, it becomes less *The Hills*, more *The Hills Have Eyes*. My destination is a backpackers' hostel just outside of Nimbin, the lawless epicentre of the Australian hippie movement.

I wait all of twenty seconds after check-in before announcing to the other residents of my hostel that 'oh, I'm not on holiday, no, I'm a *writer*,' as though the twilight state of boredom and financial stress that distinguishes my career is at all different from being on a long, interminable vacation. I regret my announcement almost instantly, when a wave of hippies approach and ask me to look at their poetry.

Freelance writers don't have many professional certainties, but when someone tells me, 'Oh, I'm a writer too', I feel the same sinking feeling that doctors at dinner parties must feel when they hear, 'Is this lump something to worry about?'

One of the poets, Sandy, is relentless – turkey-like – in her insistence that I read her dream journal, and that I also meet and write an article on her psychic guru.

Sandy is one of a handful of permanent residents of the hostel, people who came to visit Nimbin and never got around to leaving. Some are young, surly, jailbird types from country towns, but most are older women with flowing silver hair and the friendly but confused demeanour of those whose inner landscapes have been eroded by acid. They, without exception, have come to Nimbin because it is 'a place of healing'. The healing process, as far as I can tell, involves smoking cones in front of the Discovery Channel. 'I came here because I'm a free spirit,' Sandy tells me, thumb-screwing a mix into her cone and turning up the volume on a repeat of *River Monsters*.

Sandy is everywhere I go, waiting at the shower block in the morning, sitting out the front of cafes in town where I go to interview sources, next to the wood heater where I type up my notes at night. She catches me at dawn on my last morning in Nimbin, when I'm up to watch the sunrise.

I'm standing on the back lawn of the farmhouse waiting for the light. As the gloom retreats, a murky shape in the dark resolves into a Shetland pony that wanders over to me and sniffs my hand. I reach out to stroke its mane, golden-brown in the rising light. The pony whinnies and startles me out of a reverie, and I look up to see Sandy emerging from her room. I duck down behind the pony, burying my face in its mane and hoping that Sandy has missed me. The mane is soft against my cheek, and my heart is full of gratitude for this noble beast of burden that is taking time out from its morning to hide me from the predatory hippie. It is for naught. After a moment's silent commune with the pony, Sandy sees me and rushes over to tell me the news.

'I've spoken to my guru!' she announces joyfully, extending her arms for an embrace. 'And she has had a vision that you have come to tell the world about her!' I look forlornly over her shoulder, trying to calculate my chances of escaping unhugged. Sandy is older than me, but has the agility and alarming upper-body strength of the yoga-fit, so I decide against trying to fight.

'Okay,' I acquiesce. 'This guru of yours, what does she do exactly?'

'Oh, everything,' Sandy assures me, in a tone of breathless joy I last heard from a pimp in a morally unsound part of the world. 'Astrology, tarot and psychometry, and she's a clairvoyant! What's the matter? You look like you need a squeeze!' Sandy tightens her dictatorial embrace and drags me, more or less willingly, to see her Psychic.

The Psychic starts our spiritual connection by handing me a pamphlet. It's printed on pink paper and lists the psychic and spiritual services she offers, and it notes that she is 'available for parties and private readings'. Her skin is sun-damaged, her jewellery gaudy, but her smile is unexpectedly warm and her manner sharp. I was expecting some kind of new-age dipshit, and I was braced for a tone-deaf lecture on permaculture and soul-attunement, but The Psychic seems extremely switched on.

We talk for a little while about her powers and how they work, then she offers to 'do a reading' on me. Before she begins drawing the tarot cards, she lays down some fundamentals: 'The cards show only what the possibilities are. They show you a path you can take to achieve the best from life.'

The first card is Death. It tumbles out from the deck as I cut it and falls across the table between us. The angle it falls on means that the cowled figure of Death, as he rides into frame on horseback, has a rakish tilt. The Psychic doesn't miss a beat. 'Death represents the end of a cycle, and the transition into a new state of regeneration and growth.'

'So Death doesn't mean, you know, death?'

'No, no,' she says. 'It means that you've been hanging on to trauma.' She takes my hand and squeezes it. 'And it's time to let that go.' Despite itself, my calcified little heart warms to her.

I don't want to like The Psychic. I mistrust spiritualists. Not because I don't believe in earth visitors and soul retrieval and all the rest, but because they have fostered an industry of hucksters and frauds who prey on the feeble-minded, the gullible and the mad. As a child of the counterculture, I was often surrounded by the kind of grimy, dishwater Buddhists who twice a year attend ConFest (a bush party billed as 'Australia's largest outdoor alternative lifestyle festival' and possibly the southern hemisphere's greatest convergence of naked white skin, dreadlocks and giardia) in order to meet new generations of naive teen hippies who will pay them $120 to clean their aura and later relieve them of their virginity in a tent. Like knowledge, like power, a little mysticism can be a dangerous thing.

When The Psychic asks me if I believe in reincarnation I tell her no, which she bulldozes right over without acknowledging that she's heard me. She tells me I'm holding a karmic debt from a past life in which I had great power and used it selfishly; I was a great intellectual or a priest, and, also, 'probably a paedophile'.

Because of this, I have several dark spirits that follow me through life, although she tells me not to worry, because I have light spirits too. The trick, apparently, is to manage this pantheon through 'kind and positive action'. 'Have you fathered a child recently?' she asks. 'That's the fastest way to heal your karmic imbalance and banish the dark spirits.'

Several times she mentions that once I've banished my dark spirits, my 'powers will become unlimited' and a new 'carefree gypsy life will begin'. I ask her if I should father the child before or after my new gypsy life begins. 'Immediately,' she insists. 'Father the child immediately.'

'Should this be with my current partner? Because I won't see her for a few days.'

'What's her star sign?'

'I don't know.'

'What's her birthday?'

'I'm not sure.'

The Psychic pauses, looks up and breaks character.

'Oh, god,' she cackles. 'How long have you been with her? Three years? That's the worst thing I've ever heard! Learn her fucking birthday!'

After the reading, The Psychic gives me a final affirmation and assures me that my time is coming, 'in a very big way.' When I ask her if I should worry about my dark spirits, she shrugs. 'We all have travelling companions in life, good and bad. The important thing is to do good in the world,' she says. 'And find out when your girlfriend's birthday is.'

Back in Melbourne, writing the story for the Very Important Magazine, I feel as though I've absorbed some of The Psychic's optimism. As I work on the piece, one affirmation, that *my time is coming in a big way*, keeps returning to me. As I write, I start to feel better and better about the piece, better than I have writing other stories, more sure of my abilities than I've ever been, as though some kind of ethereal travelling companion is along for the ride.

A light-headed giddiness that's been with me since Nimbin grows stronger as my fingers fly over the keys. My anxieties about living up to the Magazine's standards fade, and I grow more and more at ease with the hours spent writing, sloughing off evil spirits with an almighty loofah of self-belief. I spend days straight at the computer, as my commissioned five thousand-word article becomes eight thousand, then ten thousand, then fifteen thousand words. I spend so long typing that my left eye starts twitching, and several times when I get up from the desk, my knees give out and I stumble. At one point, I trip and fall down the back stairs. No matter; I dust myself off and return to work. The only distraction is an itching ache just above the nape of my neck that grows more pronounced as the days pass.

Then, after about a week, I file the story for the Magazine and scratch the back of my head, and my hand comes away covered in blood.

At the doctor's, the GP checks my vitals and asks if I've been feeling funny lately. I tell him about the confusion, weakness and disorientation. An X-ray reveals that I've fractured my ankle falling down the stairs – I've been walking on it, oblivious, for days. He asks if anyone noticed that my speech was slurred, and if not, why not. I'm not sure how to answer that. Didn't my increasingly erratic behaviour over the past week raise alarm bells? Do my loved ones just expect me to slur and babble and pratfall occasionally? If so, it's hardly fair that they get mad when I forget their birthdays.

The doctor does a few more routine checks – reflexes, heartbeat, eyes, nose and throat – then looks at the back of my head and screams, not something you want your doctor to do, necessarily. There's a moment of silence, and he says, 'I think we're going to need a second opinion.' I wait patiently in the room for a minute, listening to hushed voices in the hallway, before two other doctors enter the room. The second looks at the back of my head and, after a moment's thought, says, 'I'm going to have to google that.'

After a few minutes, during which several doctors enter the room and huddle around a computer monitor gasping and giggling, and I manage, even through my tranquillised state, to become embarrassed in a panicked kind of way, one of them approaches me with a scalpel and a cup of dry ice. As he works, he makes conversation.

'Have you been out bush lately?'

'I was in Nimbin,' I admit. The tip of a pair of forceps grazes my scalp.

'Have you been near any livestock?'

'No. Yes,' I admit. 'I hugged a pony.'

'Yes, that would do it.'

There's a wrenching pull to the back of my head, and then the doctor brings the forceps around to show me the tick that's been burrowing into my brainstem for the past week.

For the next hour, the doctor uses dry ice and a pair of magnifying goggles to clean and disinfect the back of my head, and removes the family of ticks that have colonised it. The Psychic would be proud. I have not only fostered a child but raised an entire brood.

In the following weeks, I will require surgery to remove a cyst, an immune reaction to where the tick's bite – in addition to releasing paralysing neurotoxin straight into my nervous system – has created a near-fatal bacterial infection, which has, unbeknown to me, distracted by the deadline for the Very Important Magazine, knocked out the lymph nodes on one side of my body and strayed dangerously close to entering my brain.

While the doctor works on me, across the city, the editor of the Very Important Magazine is reading my piece of tick-addled gibberish, and deciding to spike it. When I get home there will be an email letting me know they aren't running the piece I'd pinned my dreams, financial and otherwise, on, and offering me a kill fee.

But I don't die, so The Psychic's sunny optimism was not all misplaced. And I can't feel anything – literally, I'm partially paralysed – but relieved, as the doctor shows me my new travelling companion, my little spirit animal, and crushes it between his fingers.

From Mistakes Were Made *by Liam Pieper*
(Penguin Australia Pty Ltd 2015)

REBECCA SHAW

10 Films to Watch While the Patriarchy Burns

‘One day, while trying to make Tony smile, she shows him an iron. He has never seen one before and thinks it is hysterical, along with poor people in general. But when he picks up the iron, his laughter dies. It feels … right.’

127 Hours of Mansplaining

Erin Ralston is a legendary explorer who goes canyoneering alone in order to escape what she calls the 'MENdane' city life. We know something bad will happen to her, because that is just too clever for her own good. She is rappelling through canyons in what is an obvious metaphor for vaginal birth, when suddenly she slips and falls and a huge boulder falls on her arm, trapping her. We don't know what this is a metaphor for.

After two days of captivity, there seems to be little hope that she will ever free herself. She names the boulder 'The Patriarchy' and makes a joke about it 'crushing her'. This is so clever that now we know she is surely going to die. Suddenly, she hears a man's voice! For once in her life, Erin is overjoyed to see a man, especially because this one is carrying both water and a jackhammer.

As he begins freeing her, the man – let's call him Chad – starts to explain things to her. Chad tells her where canyons come from, what canyoneering is, and what boulders are made of. He explains to her what America is. As he launches into a detailed explanation of how she ended up trapped and why this is definitely her fault, Erin deliberately pulls the boulder down onto her own head, killing herself instantly. This is widely regarded as her cleverest move yet.

TransformHers: Age of Extinctmen

It's five years after the battle between Deceptivemen and Fembots levelled Chicago and made everybody super-suspicious of their cars. The government now believes ALL robots are a threat (somehow not convinced by the #notallrobots hashtag created by the male robots who totally started the battle) and secretly dispatches a crack squad of CIA agents to destroy every last one. Cade Yeager, somehow a real character name not made up for this parody, stumbles upon OptiMs Prime disguised as an old truck, and together they set out to eliminate the robot hunters as well as the Deceptivemen who have taken over the government. They also destroy the rest of men on earth just to be safe. Cade, seeing the beautiful utopia this creates, decides to sacrifice himself for the greater good. The way he achieves this is too horrendous to depict on screen, but from that point on his method is forever known as the 'Yeager Bomb'.

Finding Men? No!

A community of beautifully animated clownfish enjoy a simple, carefree life in the beautiful surrounds of the Great Barrier Reef. Everything is going swimmingly until a team of scuba divers capture all of the male clownfish and take them back to a pet store where they are sold to ungrateful seven-year-olds who really just want a puppy. The female clownfish shrug their fishy shoulders and continue going about their fishy business. The clownfish population slowly begins to die out, but they all agree: it was totally worth it.

Not All Men in Black

After being spotted at a Richard Dawkins fan event, James Edwards – AKA Reddit user 'Fedora the Explorer 6969' – is recruited by the secret government agency Not All Men in Black, which was set up to police conversations between women all over the world. The newly monikered Agent J becomes one of the NAMIB's most prized agents, known for his incredible ability to derail any conversation two women are having simply by ignoring their personal experiences and thoughts.

But things go awry for Agent J when he makes the fateful error of accidentally listening to a woman's point of view and experiencing what he later discovers is 'empathy', which he works out by typing the words 'feelings' and 'others' point of view' into Google. The NAMIB internet monitor reports him to his superiors, and he is quickly neuralised. Empathy is for chicks.

Guardians of the 'Gal'-axy

Massive dickhead Peter 'Starlord' Quill finds himself the object of a galaxy-wide bounty hunt after stealing a mysterious orb coveted by Ronan Keating, the leader of Boyzone. Boyzone is a planet where women aren't allowed, conquered in 2014 by the participants of Gamergate when society unreasonably demanded that they treat women as if they were human. Neither of the men actually knows what the orb is for, but they still want it with every fibre of their being because another man covets it, and it is shaped like a breast. In order to fight Ronan, Quill is forced into an uneasy alliance with a big guy, a raccoon guy, a tree guy, and Gamora, a woman he wants to sleep with because she is literally the only female character in the film.

Ronan and Quill fight over the orb, eventually causing it to split open. They realise too late that it contains within it the power of every woman in the cosmos and it immediately destroys any man who is too weak to handle their strength. Ronan and Peter both die, along with every person on planet Boyzone. The tragedy is deemed an overall success.

Afterwards, Gamora is given her own movie that depicts a world where women are given the lead in superhero movies and have their picture on all the merchandise, but it is deemed 'too farfetched'.

Dawn from Baby-Sitters Club of the Planet of the Apes

War has broken out between a community of genetically evolved apes living in San Francisco's Muir Woods and the few remaining human survivors of a virus pandemic. A peaceful resolution cannot be reached because the apes have evolved to exactly match the intellectual imprint of a human male: the ego. Alternate Officer of the Baby-Sitters Club, Dawn Schafer, is parachuted in because she is originally from California, a fact that she never shuts up about. She is wearing the outfit that the other members of the Baby-Sitters Club insist on calling 'California Casual', even though they are definitely just regular clothes.

After she arrives, Dawn first sees if she can babysit her way to a peaceful solution. She cannot. Then, as a last resort, Malcolm (the human leader) and Caesar (the ape leader) are locked in a room with Dawn. For hours she lectures them about recycling and world peace and the importance of pesco-vegetarianism until they both agree to do whatever she wants, whatever anyone wants, please god just let them out of there. A truce is reached.

Ironing Man

It's been six months since the events of *Avengers: Age of Ultron*, in which the Avengers figured out how old Ultron was or something – I don't know, that movie was like super boring. Bereft of a world-ending catastrophe to worry about, Tony Stark is going through an existential crisis. Like most middle-aged men, he doesn't know if being a genius billionaire philanthropist inventor superhero is enough to keep him fulfilled. He feels as empty as the explanation of how the Hulk's pants stay on when he transforms from a thirty-inch waist to a two hundred-inch one in the space of about three seconds.

Pepper Potts is worried about Tony and about the likelihood that people are laughing at her name behind her back. One day, while trying to make Tony smile, she shows him an iron. He has never seen one before and thinks it is hysterical, along with poor people in general. But when he picks up the iron, his laughter dies. It feels … right.

He begins to iron every piece of clothing in their house, even Pepper Potts' Pleated Purple Pencil Pants, a notoriously difficult item that she is also convinced people may be laughing at. But Tony is a natural, and he loves it. In fact, he refuses to call it an 'ironing board' because he knows he will never be 'bored' again. Pepper runs his company while Tony is happy to stay at home and destroy the concept of gender roles, just like he once destroyed three-quarters of Manhattan.

Boylent Green

It's 2022, and the masses now subsist on a plankton-based product called Soylent Red. Huge babyman Detective Frank Thorn complains the loudest because he isn't getting enough protein to build huge arms that will impress other straight men at the gym – essentially a living nightmare.

One fine day, while watching the movie *One Fine Day* and not crying at all, Thorn sees an ad for a new protein-heavy product called Soylent Green. Its tagline is 'Soylent Green, ProTeen'. With both suspicion and interest piqued by this fun spelling of 'protein', Thorn decides to investigate, just like his hero Jessica Fletcher would have. Grabbing his best crime-solving hat and favourite Angela Lansbury mask, Thorn stows away in a garbage truck (where all men belong) on its way to the Soylent factory.

Once inside, he discovers the horrific truth: Soylent Green is made out of 100 per cent real teenage boys. Before he has time to post about it on Tumblr, Thorn is captured by the feminazis running the factory. As he is carried away to be fed into the meat grinder, he screams, 'YOU MUST TELL EVERYONE! SOYLENT GREEN IS MADE FROM BOYS! AND IT SHOULD BE CALLED BOYLENT GREEN, WHICH IS MUCH CLEVERER!'

But his screams go unanswered, and later on everyone agrees that Detective Frank Thorn truly was the most delicious boy of all.

World War Zzz

A hideous plague is sweeping the world. It takes mere minutes for the infected to start transforming into a self-important, middle-aged bigmouth, and less than an hour before they become entitled, pompous windbags who just want to tell women about their newest property investment in Sydney, and how they should dress so that they won't be attacked by men. The infected contaminate those around them by boring them into a stupor from which they awake a 'zzzombie'.

A team of female scientists struggles to develop an antidote that will save humanity from the unstoppable scourge. They make an exciting breakthrough, ascertaining that DNA samples from middle-aged men who ask long and self-involved questions at literary events (that turn out to not even be questions but just explanations of something they did twenty years ago) were somehow cross-contaminated in a laboratory and then fed to patient zero: Tony Abbott.

But the excitement slowly turns to dread as the scientists realise that the zzzombies were willingly voted into power at the last election and have now cut all funding for the antidote. After a brief meeting, the scientists begin working on a suicide pill instead.

Ghostbusters

It's *Ghostbusters*, but with women. Stick that in your dicks, men.

CHRIS TAYLOR

Worth a Thousand Words

‘As I was quickly informed, the Readers’ Wives page is a popular staple of the stick mag genre: a section devoted to amateur snaps of lusty women sent in by their proud-as-punch husbands. In the office it was known colloquially as the ‘Old Slappers Page’.’

At the airport, whenever called upon to state my occupation on the departure card, I'm never entirely sure what to put down. 'Comedian' doesn't feel accurate. 'Satirist' feels too pretentious. And 'Perpetual Disappointment to Gerard Henderson' feels a tad too niche. So in the end I usually just opt for the simplicity of 'Writer'. It's not altogether untrue, and, if I was being honest with you, I quite like the way it makes me sound.

For as long as I can remember, I wanted to be a writer. Attending plays as a young boy, I was always less interested in the actors getting laughs on stage than the person responsible for putting the jokes in their mouths. My bedroom walls were adorned with posters of Alan Ayckbourn and Michael Frayn. After school I played with my Alan Bennett action figure for hours. But it would be many, many years before I was ever afforded the chance to write professionally myself.

After completing an Arts degree at university, I was obligatorily unemployed for nearly two years. I was turned down for everything, including a proofreading job at the *Yellow Pages*, where my Honours degree in English Literature was judged to be an insufficient qualification for the task of checking whether Aardvark Electrics had the correct number of 'a's in its name. I was even rejected by a boating and fishing trade journal whose editor thought my experience in university publications might turn the title into a socialist mouthpiece.

'It'll be red emperors and rainbow fish every issue with you lot,' he barked. 'Your mob's the reason we had to stop using the term "jewfish" in print. Fucking "mulloway" ... what a joke!'

But my fortunes eventually changed when I was granted an interview for a junior editorial position on *Picture* magazine. At the time I hadn't actually heard of *Picture*, but the references in the job ad to wanting someone 'cheeky' and 'open-minded' made it pretty clear that it wasn't exactly *The New Yorker*. I popped down to a newsagent (for this was the pre-Google era) and found a disturbingly well-thumbed copy of the mag sandwiched in the adult section between *Mayfair* and *Hustler*. Even by porn standards, I could tell that *Picture* was decidedly downmarket: cheap-looking girls, poor quality paper, and an overabundance of exclamation marks on the cover. 'What would Alan Bennett think?' I kept asking myself. But I knew I didn't really have a choice. It was the first job interview I'd been offered in months, so I made my way to the ACP offices and rode the elevator to the seventh floor, ready to sell my soul.

Nothing whatsoever surprised me about the magazine's offices. Staffed exclusively by men, and not the kind you'd ever call dashing or athletic, the copy area choked under the clutter of proofs, snack food and smut. Cubicle partitions were studded with bawdy cartoons or humorous newspaper headlines that featured the same surname as the cubicle's occupant ('Vaughan vows to go all the way'). Collins dictionaries jostled for desk space with old back issues of *Viz*, and it was impossible to walk anywhere without encountering an acrid waft of instant coffee and cigarette smoke, both bizarrely still legal to enjoy indoors at the time.

The interview process itself was surprisingly rigorous. Far from wanting to have a chat, the magazine's editor led me into a small room and asked me to sit three separate writing tests:

1) The Synonym Challenge, where I was given one minute to write down as many variations as I could on the word 'jism'.

2) The Caption Challenge. This time I was given five minutes to devise a humorous caption for a photo of two naked women roasting a pig. 'And please don't go the spit roast angle,' advised the editor. 'It's too obvious. We're looking for people who can be one step ahead of the reader.' I can't remember exactly what I wrote, but I think it included the header 'BOAAR BLIMEY!!!', which impressed the panel.

3) The Story Challenge, where forty-five minutes were allotted to coming up with a half-page story based on a series of photos sent in by a loyal pervert, depicting his recent Halloween-themed orgy. I crammed my story full of terrible house-style puns, mostly of the 'trick or teat' variety; and I lost count of how many times I referred to breasts as 'pumpkins'. But whatever I did, it obviously worked, because I got the job.

I was officially a writer.

Right from the get-go, it was a baptism of fire. On my first day I got caught up in a crisis editorial meeting convened to resolve a dispute between the copy editor and the photo editor over the correct spelling of the word 'BAZOOKA-RAMA'. It was to be the bold-splash header for a double-page spread about girls who like guns, but no one could agree on how it should be spelled. The copy editor was arguing strongly for two hyphens, so it would read as 'BAZOOK-A-RAMA'. Pictorial insisted there was no room for a second hyphen in the layout.

'But it just doesn't look right without one!' pleaded Copy. 'We'd never write "JUGSA-RAMA". We'd write "JUGS-A-RAMA".'

'Yeah, but "bazooka" already has an "A" built into it, so a second "A" is redundant,' replied Pictorial, with an astute sense of logic that you wouldn't necessarily expect from someone wearing a 'No Fat Chicks' T-shirt. 'Besides, what about that issue we did in May with the "VAGINA-GO-GO" header?'

This kind of back-and-forth intransigence went on for at least another two hours. At one point the copy editor threatened to set fire to his overflowing in-tray of World's Dirtiest Jokes if he didn't get his way. But ultimately, *Picture* magazine being what it is, pictures won the day. The copy editor graciously consented to a single hyphen on the grounds that it was impossible to lay the word up with two hyphens without obscuring a breast somewhere along the way.

'It's what the readers would have wanted,' he conceded.

My principal responsibility at the magazine was to look after the Readers' Wives page. I'd never heard the term 'readers' wives' before, and my initial, naive reaction was to assume that this otherwise prurient journal might also cater to literary tastes by profiling the female muses of respected men of letters. I half-expected to find polite Q&As with the spouses of Dinny O'Hearn or Jason Steger. But I couldn't have been more wrong. It was just more tits and muff, only not quite as well lit.

As I was quickly informed, the Readers' Wives page is a popular staple of the stick mag genre: a section devoted to amateur snaps of lusty women sent in by their proud-as-punch husbands. In the office it was known colloquially as the 'Old Slappers Page'. The women were typically over forty, and commonly on the tubby side. Almost always, they were photographed squatting naked on a bed, or clutching their breasts, in a clumsy approximation of poses they'd copied from the professionals.

We used to receive between thirty and forty photo submissions a week. A reader named Arthur used to send in pics of his beloved wife, Ginger, every single week. Ginger was well into her sixties, but, on the evidence available, had lost none of her enthusiasm for amateur soft porn. Each week a new A4 envelope would arrive with fresh pictures of Ginger in all her domestic, undraped glory. She was variously photographed nude with a vacuum cleaner, nude with a watering can, nude with a rolling pin and, in a curious twist on the housekeeping theme, nude with a cardboard cut-out of Whoopi Goldberg from the film *Sister Act*.

Arthur's photographic studies of Ginger had never once found their way into the magazine, but it was hard not to admire his persistence. What I'd initially dismissed as a rather sad, tawdry relationship, I later grew to accept as harmless at worst, and rather touching at best: here was a husband still sufficiently enamoured and turned on by his wife to want to place her in the pages of *Picture*, which, in his universe, was the highest pedestal there was.

And that's how I came to regard all the readers' wives. Or it was, at least, until the life-stopping day when I opened up an envelope to find pictures of my mother.

My nude, raw, butt-naked mother.

There she was, the woman who'd packed my playlunch for years, splayed across a queen-size bed, vagina-side up.

'Who's the hottie?' asked the editor, looking over my shoulder.

'I'm ... not sure,' I said. 'I don't think we'll run it.'

'You kidding me?' he said. 'With cans like that? She's good enough to go pro.'

I couldn't believe what was happening. *My own mother.* This was the woman who was so prudish that she used to leave the room during the love scenes on *Chances*, and now here she was with her baps out like Mosman's answer to Samantha Fox.

I checked the back of the envelope for the sender's name. Gunther Pippos, it said. Who the hell was Gunther Pippos?! Was Mum having an affair with a kinky dago? She traditionally hated foreigners, so this was becoming more out of character by the minute. An enclosed note from Gunther, written by hand in a disarmingly formal cursive and accompanied by sprigs of dried lavender and linseed, said: 'I hope you enjoy these portraits of my saucy Marina.'

Marina? I could still think straight enough to know that that wasn't my mother's name. I went back through the photos a second time and, under a less shell-shocked scrutiny – and to my profound relief – it became gut-soothingly clear that my mother hadn't become an erotic model after all. She merely had a doppelganger. The order of the universe had been restored.

Or so I thought.

Roughly a week later, at the point in the production cycle when I had to sign off on which Readers' Wives had made the cut, the photos of Marina were missing in action. I couldn't find them anywhere. No matter how thoroughly I searched the piles of lewd refuse that littered my desk, they simply couldn't be located.

'Is this her?' suggested a colleague, joining in the hunt.

'No, that's Whoopi Goldberg,' I said. 'Not even close.'

'Have you been through your trays?'

'Yes.'

'IN tray and OUT tray?'

'I've been through every fucking tray. They're not here.'

'Well, just go with someone else,' he said. 'You must have tonnes of other options.'

Going with someone else had already occurred to me, but Marina had been such a huge hit around the office, especially with the editor, that questions would be asked of my editorial judgement if I didn't include her. I was still relatively new at the magazine, and keen to make a good impression, so the way I saw it I really only had one option left if I was to give the bosses what they wanted.

Nervously, I picked up the phone and dialled my mother's number.

'Hello?'

'Hi, it's Chris. I'm in a spot of trouble at work.'

'What do you mean – are you okay?'

'Yeah, no, I'm fine,' I assured her. 'I just need to ask you a slightly weird favour. I don't want you to freak out or anything, but I'm wondering if I can come over to take some photos of you.'

'Of *me*?!'

'For the magazine, yeah. They'd be very tasteful. And we wouldn't need to tell Dad.'

'What *sort* of photos?' she asked.

'I need you to be a reader's wife ... I've lost some photos of our hero wife, see, and you look exactly like her. In fact, when I first saw her, I thought it *was* you. Which is a compliment, really. So I just thought ...'

'You want me,' she interrupted, 'to pose nude in your magazine? Is that what you're asking me?!'

The second she said it, I knew how ridiculous the idea had been. Was I seriously proposing to go round and take photographs of my naked mother? Too humiliated to explain further, I hung up, muttering a sheepish apology, and buried my head in my hands. 'What would Alan Bennett think?' I once again asked myself over and over.

Resigned to submitting a substitute wife in place of Marina, I started sifting through the various candidates on my desk. As I moved the Whoopi Goldberg pic to one side to create some space, I suddenly had a wild idea.

Ginger! Ginger could maybe – just *maybe* – pass for Marina if we shot the photos cleverly. Her face wasn't especially similar, but her body was a reasonably good match, so I figured with a brown wig and some cunning lighting we might just get away with it. Once again I reached for the phone.

'Hello, is that Arthur?' I asked.

'Yes.'

'Hello, it's Chris Taylor from *Picture* magazine. I'm ringing up about Ginger.'

'Oh, right, yes. So you got the photos I sent you then?'

'Yes, we've been getting them for the past year …'

'Smashing bird, isn't she? Sixty-two years old, and still the best rig I've ever seen.'

'Yes, it's very impressive.'

'And all her own bits,' he boasted further. 'No fakies in this house. All-natural jubblies, as real as the day God gave them to her.'

'Great, which is why I'm ringing, in a way,' I said. 'I'm wondering if Ginger's free this afternoon to do a photo shoot.'

'But I've already sent you the pictures.'

'And they're all great, really. It's just that we have a new brief from the magazine that's quite specific, so we'll need to take some new shots.'

'Well, she's on the dialysis machine at the moment,' he said. 'What time are you thinking?'

'Whatever suits, really, but it does need to be today.'

'Do you need any props? I've got a new mop which might be quite good. Why don't you swing by after three? I'll get her in the mood for you.'

Arriving at the appointed time, I was greeted on the porch by Arthur, who appeared slightly more distinguished than I was expecting. Wearing sensible slacks and a polo shirt, he looked more like someone who was about to play eighteen holes than someone who was about to order his naked wife onto all-fours.

'Cup of tea?' he offered.

He was really quite the gentleman. Their home was by no means flash, but nor was it untasteful. Fresh flowers occupied the dining-room vases and, without exception, the oil paintings on the walls were originals, not prints. Arthur wasn't lying when he said there were 'no fakies in this house'. The living room was dominated by some bulky medical machinery, beside which stood a grotesque goddess in her dressing gown, flashing a leg that was all too familiar to me.

'Where do you want me?' the famous Ginger purred.

It was clear almost immediately that this wasn't going to work. In the flesh, Ginger looked nothing like Marina. Even with the addition of the brunette wig, you couldn't escape the feeling that she looked more like a character that Matt Lucas might play, rather than someone any self-respecting *Picture* reader would want to beat off to. But it wasn't my place to spoil their fantasy. Not now. Not after I'd raised their hopes so high.

'Shall we start in the bedroom or the shower?' enquired Arthur, relishing his self-appointed role as co-director. 'I've got a toilet brush, feather duster, hedge clippers – whatever you need, just sing out.'

The shoot lasted just over an hour, alternately lurching from the monstrous to the comical, but only in my eyes. Arthur and Ginger had never had it so good. The pleasure on their faces was unmistakable: Arthur beaming with pride, Ginger glowing with joy.

'So, which issue should we keep an eye out for, then?' asked Arthur, as he saw me into my cab.

'Hard to say,' I replied. 'That stuff's not really up to me.'

'But you promise they *will* be published this time,' he said. 'It would mean the world to her.'

'I'll do my best,' I promised. And I really did mean it.

Racing back to Park Street to meet my deadline, I resolved to include the shots of Ginger in my layout submission, regardless of how ludicrous the photos might look. I dropped the film off on level two, where the photo lab traditionally looked after the *Bulletin*, but the assistants were always happy to moonlight for *Picture* because it was a nice change of pace from developing snaps of John Howard.

To this day I can't explain why I didn't just come clean with the editors and explain the whole sorry farce. I tell myself that it was because I was anxious about looking incompetent, but part of me now wonders whether I thought Ginger had a natural right to be in the magazine, alongside the other wives. Whatever my motives, when I presented my final proofs featuring Ginger's carnival smile in the place where everyone was expecting Marina's snatch, I was fired on the spot. It wasn't heated. It wasn't dramatic. It was simply the moment when my editor accurately deduced that my passion for soft porn was no more real than my aptitude for it.

But he let me keep the proofs. And a week or so later, I slid them under the door of Arthur and Ginger's house, where I like to think they enjoy pride of place alongside all of the other originals on their walls.

FIONA SCOTT-NORMAN

Good English
Stock

‘Everything was clotted and rich, pan-fried and creamy, crispy on the outside, moist on the inside, and unapologetically saturated with animal fat and brandy.’

T he happiest memories I have of Dad are from when he had one hand up inside a dead bird's cavity. Good gravy, he lived to cook. That wouldn't surprise if the Scott-Normans had been Italian, Jewish, or any of those enviably demonstrative cultures where people speak with their hands, hug regularly and express love via a groaning table and the phrase 'Eat! Eat!' But the Scott-Normans are from good English stock. And England is a nation that expresses love by silently delivering you a cup of tea, struggling facially with its emotions, and then withdrawing apologetically.

Not even on a good day is England renowned for its cuisine. In the 1970s, when Arthur Scott-Norman was at the height of his powers, the apogee of British haute cuisine was the shrimp cocktail. No one ever says, 'Let's go out for an English.' Well, they do, but only inasmuch as the most popular dish in Britain today is Indian. Chicken tikka masala was reputedly created in Glasgow in 1971, by adding leftover tomato soup to a curry that a disgruntled bus driver had complained was 'dry'. It's hardly the stuff that dreams and Michelin-starred restaurants are made of.

For the lion's share of the 20th century, the English diet consisted of soggy brussels sprouts; reimagined offal; steamed swede; boiled turnip; creamed fish pie; a scrape of dripping on toast; and baked beans, spam, fried eggs, spam, chips, spam and spam. Whatever spam is. [Insert emoticon for shrugging right here.] Britain's love affair with the whodunnit probably springs from its surfeit of mystery meats: haggis, luncheon meat, black pudding, brawn, chitterlings, meat paste and faggots. Yes, faggots are a thing. Yes, Dad loved them.

Even today, despite the best efforts of nutrition crusader Jamie Oliver, the historical reputation of British cooking still lingers dismally in the air, like the smell of boiled cabbage in a seaside B&B. Judge not, though. The UK had a solid four decades of war effort, belt-tightening and privation to deal with. There's not much chef-tastic triumph to be had when your pantry is bare but for a pig lung, stale bread, no herbs and powdered egg. A *Masterchef* World War II mystery box challenge; now there's something I'd watch.

That my dad rose like a culinary phoenix from the poverty cuisine of war rationing is a testament, really, to the human spirit. I imagine him standing in the midst of Blitz-torn London – a time when the only item with nutritional value not already rationed was dirt, and bread could only be sold a day old so that people weren't encouraged to eat it – shaking his fist at the sky, a latter-day trans-Atlantic Scarlett O'Hara, crying, 'As God is my witness, I will never go hungry again!'

Dad's lifelong quest for good mouthfeel and fine ingredients was also spurred by his service in the RAF as a crash site investigator, an experience that left him deeply scarred and permanently phobic about carrots.

The story, as family legend has it, goes something like this: there came a time during World War II when the Brits had a breakthrough with radar. All of a sudden they were shooting down masses of German planes, and felt it would be smart to send Jerry off in another direction. So RAF personnel – all of them – were fed carrots at every meal, morning, noon and night, and ordered to eat them. The implication was that the high doses of Vitamin A gave the pilots such extraordinary vision that they could down a Focke in the dark with the naked eye.

A contemporary nutritionist might note that carrots boiled for half an hour have all the nutritional value of wind, but the German high command was confounded for a while, certainly long enough for Dad to consume his lifetime supply of carrots. Never ate another one – and he lived to eighty-nine. He was a man of his convictions, my father. He also went to the grave having refused to ever watch a single American film or TV programme, because he was disgusted with them for taking so long to enter the war. Say what you like about Arthur, but he could hold a fucking grudge.

He could also, excuse my French, fucking cook. In today's parlance, Arthur owned the kitchen, and what came out of it was nearly always delicious. (Nearly – I've never forgotten nor forgiven tripe-and-onion-gate, when my refusal to eat a rubbery mess of bleached cow's stomach for dinner led to it being served up cold for breakfast.)

Dad was of medium height, handsome when young, and, from mid-life on, as stout as the proverbial barrel of ale. He cut an old-fashioned figure: think Friar Tuck or Henry VIII; a man of means, of appetites, of substance. His bulk lent him gravitas, and, later in life, when coupled with his white beard and penetrating blue eyes, allowed him to play Santa with zero preparation and a high degree of credibility. I'd chide him about his stomach, which was large enough to exert a degree of gravitational pull, and he'd pat it unrepentantly and say, 'It's all paid for, Fiona.'

A safety engineer by day, by night Dad was a comfort-food black belt in the *Two Fat Ladies* tradition, complete with grease-smeared fingers and blue-and-white striped chef's apron. Everything was clotted and rich, pan-fried and creamy, crispy on the outside, moist on the inside, and unapologetically saturated with animal fat and brandy. After we moved to Australia, where the climate screams for salads, I stopped asking him for recipes because every single one, including bread, began with, 'Take a walnut-sized lump of lard.'

But in England in the 1970s, when everyone else was charring their chops to leather and sieving the grey lumps from their mashed potato, I grew up with bloody steaks and bright minted peas. I didn't know bad food existed until I went to boarding school. At home on Sunday mornings, Dad would serve up fizzing Pimm's No. 1 augmented with Cointreau in chilled pewter tankards, and Mum, Dad and I would get thoroughly sloshed en route to the roast. Which was, by the way, always outstanding. Leg of lamb with homemade mint sauce, rare roast beef and horseradish, chicken with sausage and chestnut stuffing. Not that our family had ever been church-goers, but our Sundays were a pretty sweet alternative to a hard pew and Protestant service.

Every meal, in Dad's hands, was a banquet. Mum was an excellent cook, but Dad pushed the boat out. Kippers poached in milk and butter, mushrooms sautéed in cream, lobster smothered in cheese. Fillet steak with pâté on top. Or stuffed with oysters. Or both. Stilton and port for dessert. Irish coffee. I did a gig a while ago at Melbourne's Athenaeum Club, one of those conservative men's clubs with a doorman, exclusive membership and clusters of stuffed leather armchairs where world domination is discussed in hushed tones. The menu in the dining room whooshed me back thirty years. I sat there sipping game broth with a dash of sherry – my bowl correctly tilted away, dozens of Len Deighton and John Le Carré novels eyeing me from the bookshelf – all the while thinking how very 'Dad' it was. And how no one else I knew would truly appreciate the intoxicating proximity of power and well-hung venison.

Unfortunately, sharing good times was never Arthur's long suit. He had what you could generously call 'a chef's temperament', which I would less romantically characterise as 'shouting all the fucking time'. I wonder now if he had PTSD, or was a teeny bit on the spectrum. Probably PTSD. He did, after all, spend the war digging up flash-burned body parts. As Mum, who served during the war as a nurse, once told me matter-of-factly, 'We didn't have therapy back in our day, Fiona. Some nights we still both wake up screaming.'

It was a rare meal that wasn't interrupted by Dad – bless his frustrated, high blood-pressured, impatient heart – losing his temper somewhere between boning the chicken and spooning out the gourmet ice-cream, topped with just a dribble of Frangelico. Ironically, he cooked to relax, and the mind boggles to think what he would have been like without it. The first Christmas after he died, I busted Mum out of the nursing home for the day and cooked without Dad glaring over my shoulder. It was also, it transpired, the first Christmas we'd ever had that didn't involve significant quantities of yelling. 'High five,' said Mum, raising her arm to celebrate having no need to flinch.

This was the fundamental paradox in Dad's nature. On the one hand: a generous host, a compulsive over-caterer and someone who saw hospitality as a sacred charge. On the other hand: deeply antisocial. Loved feeding people, couldn't stop shouting at them.

He had learned to make curry when he was the fire chief of Dar es Salaam in Tanzania in the late 1940s, and in my teenage years he would cook feasts from scratch (note: no tomato soup here) for up to twenty admiring guests. Arthur's curry lunches were legend, and invitations were sought-after. But after a few hours of beer, bonhomie and playing the host, he'd inevitably end up aggravated. We knew the party was over when he'd put on a bagpipe-heavy military band record and start pumping up the volume. He'd turn it louder and louder, until the level was unbearable and everybody got the hint and went home. Subtle as a smack in the face with a wet haddock.

He did not teach me to cook, in much the same way that he didn't teach Mum to drive. A few sessions of 'Jesus Christ, Norah! What the hell are you doing?' turned a nervous beginner into someone who walked away from cars for a lifetime. I couldn't stand the heat, and I stayed well out of the kitchen. Look, I eventually taught myself the basics, and he gave me his recipe for spag bol and taught me how to flip a pancake, but that was it. It's been said that when an old man dies, a library burns. Well, when Dad went, it was the Great Cooking Library of Alexandria that was razed to the ground.

I did inherit sheaves of handwritten traditional sausage recipes, which all require the rinsing of many feet of sheep gut in salt water, and contain ingredients now banned by the Food Safety Authority. But the one tenet I absorbed whole-heartedly was that having guests means feeding them rich food until their livers turn to pâté. I utterly equate hospitality with love; I know it's the best he could do.

Ultimately, among other health issues, Dad predictably developed diabetes, which he was supposed to control by diet. Ahahaha. He complied by hiding packets of biscuits around the house, and Mum, bedridden with her dicky spine, would hear a tell-tale *crinkle crinkle* emerging from the lounge room. His other technique was to buy boxes of chocolates 'for Norah', which she rarely got to eat. 'Who's been browsing?' she'd call out, after going for a Quality Street and again finding a handful of wrappers and tinfoil.

Early talk about Dad joining Norah in the nursing home evaporated when he saw what she was getting fed. I can't blame him. He saw boiled carrots in his future and put his foot down. He even lied about having applied, and sat there nodding when Mum fretted about how long it was taking to process the paperwork. A man has one great passion in his life, and with due respect to my Mum, Dad's was food.

The first date Dad took Mum on was to harvest brussels sprouts in the snow. Their honeymoon was a bust because Mum came down with something, and Dad went to the pub on his own each night and would totter back to their houseboat smelling amorously of pickled onions.

He'd drive Mum bonkers, in a ritual that neither of them had the capacity to escape, by asking her at the end of every meal what she wanted for the next one. Three times a day he would ask, and three times a day she would reply, 'Arthur, I've just eaten, I can't think about food right now.' Three squabbles a day, like clockwork.

Soon after he died, I visited Mum and noted that *Two Fat Ladies* was coming up on the telly. I figured she'd be keen to watch, but was met with a raised eyebrow and a firm headshake. 'Thank goodness,' she said, 'that I never have to watch another damn cooking show.'

Dad stood indomitable for years, holding a catalogue of ailments at bay through sheer crankiness and pottering round the kitchen. He was easy to please and a pleasure to buy for. When I flew to visit them in Toowoomba, I'd bring him hipster treats: artisanal pork pies from the farmer's market, dark chocolate, a jar of organic mango chutney. I knew he was really dying when he began to let me cook, and when I found a packet of instant mash in the pantry.

I hand-fed him his last meal in the hospital: some deep-fried cod roe, and a glass of Piper-Heidsieck bubbly, which I decanted into his hospital sippy cup. We toasted. The received wisdom is that hearing is the last sense to go, but for Dad I'd swear it was taste. Apart from anything else, he'd been deaf for years and was resolute in not turning on his hearing aids. (This meant he couldn't hear what we said, which made him cross, which meant he was justified in a bit of shouting. It was kind of genius.)

Clearing out the house, I found mounds of tinned food stockpiled in every cupboard, up to and including the master wardrobe. Dad shopped as though he was still hosting dinner parties for twenty. As though he were still on rations. There were cans of escargot, artichokes and water chestnuts. Lobster bisque and mandarins. Asparagus (green *and* white), Scotch broth and lychees, foie gras and crab meat. All bought can-by-can by a gourmand on a pension. All out of date.

I shop like Dad. Maybe even for him. I poke meat, squeeze avocados, tap melons, sniff tomatoes. I used to think he was a wanker for greeting restaurateurs by name. Now I do the same. I feel deeply uncomfortable if I don't have a pantry surplus, and I have a tin of Lyle's Golden Syrup that I've been meaning to put in a treacle tart for five years. Ten, maybe. Fortunately that gear does not go off.

I saw Dad truly happy three times. Once was watching me do comedy; from the stage I could see him doubled-up and hooting. The second time was in a photograph taken before I was born, crouched in front of the seven salmon he'd caught fishing that day in Canada. His face was lit up like Christmas, and Mum said, hands down, it was the happiest day of his life.

The third time was in Perth, in 1979. Dad had a new job with Woodside Petroleum, and he'd moved us to Australia. While my parents looked for a house, Woodside put us up at the Sheraton, which was, by Perth in 1979 standards, very, very fancy. One night at the bistro, Dad's lobster thermidor did not come out as God intended. So he did what absolutely no one does ever in a five-star hotel restaurant, which was pick up his plate and disappear for thirty minutes.

When he returned, he had a lobster thermidor, as per the book, steaming in his hands, and the kind of transcendent smile you get when you've bustled your way into an international hotel's kitchen, told the chef he's an idiot, AND COOKED YOUR OWN MEAL. Happiest. Man. In. The. World.

Oh, and one more thing I inherited. If a meal's substandard, back it goes. Boom. Thanks, Dad. Love you.

TONY MARTIN

———◦◦◦———

Follies

'The drinks arrived, and Batman sipped daintily, yet menacingly, through a long, spiralling straw.'

The Dark Knight Triumphant in Classic Cooney Farce

I t's hard to know what was going through Batman's head when he accepted the lead in the much-anticipated revival of *Run for Your Wife* at the Old Gotham Playhouse.

It had all started one evening at a benefit dinner for the Wayne Foundation. No one was too surprised when the event was gatecrashed by the Riddler; as usual, he'd been unable to resist pre-empting his appearance with a series of transparent and unfunny brain teasers posted on riddlemethis.com. As soon as the Riddler arrived, bursting from a suspiciously large cake in a flurry of puns, Batman rappelled down from a skylight and beat him yet more senseless before he could effect the advertised kidnapping. The target was Sir Marmaduke Pfogg (no relation), the famous theatre director who was fresh from a series of triumphs in Londinium's West End. Pfogg was quick to offer the caped crusader both his profound gratitude and the lead in his new play.

To change out of his bulky night-vision suit, Batman would have had to get to Bruce Wayne's office on the 915th floor. But as it was raining out, and he was facing an elaborate series of high-altitude swoops and at least one somersault through a plate-glass window, he decided to accept Pfogg's offer of a drink instead. Trailing his enormous, scissoring hang-glider wings, he repaired awkwardly to the cocktail bar. 'I'll have whatever you're having,' he rasped to the flamboyant director as the pair perched themselves on tall stools and surveyed the laminated bill of fare.

'Two Cocksucking Cowboys,' Pfogg barked at the barman, who plonked a folded napkin and a dish of complimentary nuts before the dark knight.

'Listen, Pfogg,' said Batman, maintaining his threatening croak, even as he suavely flipped cashews into his mouth. 'Why would I want to do *Run for Your Wife*?' And then, after a suitably dramatic pause, 'I'm Batman.'

The drinks arrived, and Batman sipped daintily, yet menacingly, through a long, spiralling straw.

'I know you are,' said Pfogg, placing a reassuring paw on Batman's gloved and clenched fist. 'But I think you can be so much *more*.'

The crusader looked unconvinced. Pfogg leaned in closer. 'You saw what I did with the Green Lantern in *Not Now, Darling*.'

Batman allowed himself a tight smile. *Darling* had been a smash. 'In brightest day, in blackest night … *get ready to split your sides!!!*' the headlines had screamed. 'Let those who worship evil's might, *watch this crazy farce take flight!!!*' The Lantern had stayed pretty much on-script until the finale, only using his power ring to sort out a mix-up with the hotel reservations. Equally crowd-pleasing was the Flash in *No Sex Please, We're British*; the various near-miss entrances and exits had never been executed with such lightning speed. And at the Justice League AGM, they were still talking about the Elongated Man's across-the-drawing-room brassiere removal in *Move Over, Mrs Markham*, Pfogg's most recent West End hit ('Season *stre-e-e-e-e-etched* to record twentieth week!!!'). Maybe a spell creeping the boards wasn't such a bad idea. The crowds had loved him that time he'd run for mayor against the Penguin (laughably but memorably dramatised in *Hizzoner, Dizzoner*).

'Alright, ya got me,' hissed Batman, slamming down his fellatio-themed beverage and firing a bat hook into the ceiling. 'See you at rehearsals.' And with that, he shot upwards and was gone, leaving his agent to sort out the details.

In order to comply with Equity regulations, Batman needed to at least go through the motions of an audition. He chose to recite the classic Two Ronnies 'Fork Handles' sketch, playing both parts in a hissed and threatening manner that evinced little humour and led the seen-it-all stagehands in the flies to pinch their noses and recall the Atom's disastrous Lear (the performance itself was fine, but it was only visible to one audience member at a time, hunched over a microscope for a 'bum-numbing five hours' – the *Bugle*.)

The six-week rehearsal period was constantly disrupted by the lead actor's sudden bat hook-assisted departures, supposedly to tackle some crime-related emergency, which the supporting cast increasingly chose to read as stage fright. At first, Batman seemed miscast in the role of the cockney cabbie with 'two wives, two lives and a very precise schedule for juggling them both', his massive cape repeatedly getting caught in the doors of the adjoining hotel rooms. His harshly growled ad-libs ('Bigamy is a sickness ... and I'm the cure!') and relentless beating of the gay neighbour seemed at odds with the light, frothy tone of Ray Cooney's 'naughty but nice' classic. But the scene where he cavorted in nothing but cowl and boxers was a winner, and helped to offset some mystifying references to 'Aunt Harriet' in the Act II tour de force with the ice bucket.

Throughout these rehearsals (which were plagued by the sneak attacks of various supervillains, each causing the mise en scene to deteriorate into a lengthy fistfight), Pfogg encouraged the dark knight to take part in 'trust exercises' with the rest of the company. Batman's standard response was to fling two capsules of knockout gas into the orchestra pit, summon a huge tank-like vehicle to the stage door, shatter the French doors as he hurled himself through them and repair to the prow of the Chrysler Building, where he would stand broodingly, his cape whipping against the cold Gotham night as he recited, over and over, the speech about the mix-up with the scanty panties.

The pressure of the role, not to mention the ongoing raids on the Gotham Mint by the Clock King (incongruously teamed with Olga) resulted in Batman's frequent, frustrating absences. No one was convinced the day a 'Batman' who was clearly an elderly man with a dapper moustache, much like that worn by millionaire Bruce Wayne's manservant, turned up to rehearsals sporting an even less convincing cockney accent than usual.

But somehow, come opening night, spirits were high. For the post-dress-rehearsal cast party the previous night, Batman had gassed the entire company and transported them, in the Batcopter, to his vast subterranean lair for a catered piss-up. The evening had ended with the host regaling his co-stars with several violent theatrical anecdotes, while the two actresses who played the roles of his nymphomaniac wives shot up and down on the Batpoles sans underpants.

'Break a leg, everyone,' toasted Pfogg, raising high a freshly shaken Buttfucking Bellboy, but by the time the curtain fell, two hours later, the only fractures sustained were those of three people in the front row and an unconscious Two-Face, whose surprise appearance in Act III had resulted in the show's biggest laughs as he extemporised a new scene playing two separate husbands simultaneously. Applause for the actual cast members was muted, and even the spray of flowers presented to a noticeably embarrassed Batman during the curtain call left a bitter aftertaste. Batman realised they were from Louie the Lilac just seconds before they exploded, bringing down what little remained of the scenery after the fight.

Afterwards, in the bar, Gordon and O'Hara were putting brave faces on, but the caped crusader, clutching a highball and taking small, hesitant drags on a cigarette, could read it on their faces.

'This came for you,' said the Commissioner, handing Batman a folded note. 'It's from Egghead.'

'Another threat to flood the city with albumen?' snarled the dark knight.

'I'm afraid he was reviewing tonight's show for the *Times*,' said Gordon. 'This is what he'll be filing.'

Batman raised it to his cowl, and by the time he'd finished reading the notice, which made full use of the author's penchant for egg puns, his face was taut with fury.

'"No Bernard Cribbins", am I?' he thundered. 'I'll show him whose performance is "a badly timed yolk"!'

But it was too late. By the time the *Times* hit the newsstands, the city's criminals would all be laughing at him. *Run for Your Wife* had been a mistake, Batman could see that now. He needed to put it behind him, reassert his authority, show the scum on the streets who was boss. First thing in the morning, he'd call Pfogg and say yes to *Nunsense*.

Bing Crosby and Bob Hope in *The Road* by Cormac McCarthy

When he woke in the woods in the dark and the cold of night he'd reach out and touch the figure sleeping beside him. Nights dark beyond darkness and the days more grey each one than what had gone before. Like the onset of some cold glaucoma dimming away the world. The world that was now barren, silent, godless. Without hope. Whaddaya mean without Hope? Who do you think has been pushing the damn shopping cart for the last fifteen miles? Shecky Greene?

Yes of course. I'm sorry.

He thought the month was October but he wasn't sure. Time no longer had any meaning. It could have been months since the Jack Benny cameo. Or mere days.

So, are we going to die?

Yes we're going to die. Sometime. Not now.

Worse than we did at the Copa?

Worse than that.

When it was light enough to use the binoculars he glassed the valley below. Were they being watched? Surely in this blasted lifeless glen here among the mummied dead no one would be looking for two out-of-work musicians on the run from the mob hoping to stow away on a ship to Rio.

There is no ship is there?

Go to sleep.

Head out west you said.

Be quiet.

We'll meet a coupla fabulous lookin' dames.

I'm sorry.

We're gonna be rich you said. Now I'm eating dog food out of a can.

Hush. They'll find us.

I tell you who I'd like to find. The chump who sold us this map!

They were moving south. There'd be no surviving another winter here. Hope had eaten the last of the food along with the microfilm he'd found in the Chinese fortune cookie. Although why he'd done that was no longer important. They set out along the blacktop in the gunmetal light, shuffling through the ash, each the other's world entire.

You got any water?

That broad threw the last of it in my face.

There had been others along the road. The lost, the undead, the diseased and doomed, Peter Sellers as an unhelpful Indian doctor. There were those who would do them harm. Who would come for them while they slept. And there were only so many times they could get away with the old pat-a-cake distraction routine.

Do you remember what you used to call me?

A slope-nosed schnook?

Something like that.

The clocks had stopped at 1.17. A long shear of light and a series of low concussions. Robert Morley's Girl Bombs had wreaked their terrible vengeance.

There's nothing. There's nothing left.

Whaddaya mean? I still have these French postcards.

We need water. We need food.

I need a weekend in Las Vegas!

In his dream she was sick and he cared for her. But he did not take care of her and she died alone somewhere in the dark and there is no other tale to tell. At one time he would have cried for her. Now he only wished he had kept some of the fruit piled high atop her head.

They came to trees across the road where they were forced to unload the cart and carry everything over the trunks and repack it all on the far side.

This is bad.

What, the script?

But even self-referential one-liners had ceased to have any meaning for them. Too tired even to do the 'walk this way' gag they trudged deeper into a dark gorge and came across a bridge collapsed in a dank slow-moving river.

Oh god no. What next?

A rickshaw chase?

This is it. This is where it ends.

But I haven't been slapped by a single chorus girl.

Just go. Leave me.

What?

It's alright. You'll see.

I can't.

Please.

Not without a song.

Alright then.

Heaving his exhausted partner into the cart Hope felt the flare gun snug in the pocket of his filthy coat. Sketched upon a pall of soot downstream the outline of a burnt city like a black paper scrim. Bodies melted and black amid corridors of drifting ash. Slumped within the rusting cart Crosby counted them in.

Oh, the earth is scorched,
It's all been torched,
Ain't nothin' gonna be the same.
But like this verse,
It could be worse ...
Two guys, one dame!

But there's broads no more,
No Dottie Lamour,
To help us share the load.
Round every bend a killer,
(Quick hide, it's Phyllis Diller!)
A post-apocalyptic thriller,
(It's the whole magilla!)
This picture's got no filler,
(I wrestled a gorilla!)
As we shuffle on down The Rooooooaaaad!

Hey fellas. Am I too late?
Yes Dean, you are.
Okay.
Okay then.

ROBERT SKINNER

The Art of Tour Guiding

If there is screaming and hopping and running about, smile ruefully and say, 'Welcome to the outback.' This is the most important phrase in your arsenal.

Tour guiding in Australia is easy on some levels: you feed your charges well, take them to the right places and try to keep their feet warm. But extreme weather, mechanical problems, flies in the daytime, mosquitoes at night, the Germans, the lack of sleep, the feelings of deep existential loneliness ... all these things will conspire against you.

You should never, or almost never, give your tourists the choice between two options. This is a mistake inexperienced guides often make. Are you not the leader of this expedition? Have you not been here a hundred times before and know what it's about? Don't go inflicting the misery of democracy on them. It may seem generous and noble, but in the middle of an Australian summer I have seen some people reduced to tears.

An outback tour is not a luxury cruise. A cruise liner gives the impression that everything is taken care of and available. This is impossible when you're the sole driver/guide, and it doesn't make for a good experience anyway. I prefer to give the illusion of barely contained chaos. It contributes to people's sense of adventure and togetherness. When it goes well, it will feel like you're the captain of a pirate ship.

If a family of native mice sneak on board your bus, and are only discovered when you're barrelling down the highway, don't stop. If there is screaming and hopping and running about, smile ruefully and say, 'Welcome to the outback.' This is the most important phrase in your arsenal. Keep driving if you can. Maybe shout some words of encouragement as the tourists round up the mice into saucepans.

I ran bus tours through central Australia for three years (2009 to 2012). On the first day of those tours, someone would always ask what time we were going to arrive at camp. Camp was six hundred kilometres away, and it was a good opportunity to set a few things straight.

'Look,' I'd say, 'this isn't the Deutsche Bahn. There are rogue cows, flat tyres, and headwinds like you wouldn't believe.' I'd stare wistfully out the window for a moment. 'In some ways, we'll be lucky to get there at all.'

One morning I tried to leave it at that, but the girl who asked the question just kept looking at me expectantly.

I sighed. 'What time? I dunno. About 6.30, 7?'

'Okay! Thank you!' She turned to her friend. 'He says we're arriving at 6.37.'

A tour guide should try not to say too much on the first day. A week is a long time, and you don't want to devalue your own currency. By the end of a tour, no one remembers the first day anyway. Put some music on and start driving.

An older guide once said to me, 'It's like cards. Don't throw all your aces down on the table at once. You gotta play them one at a time.' (This is a profound nugget of tour-guiding wisdom, but spectacularly bad advice for actual card games.)

A critical job for any tour guide is to bond the group. You want them to feel as though, for the next six days, they're all part of the same story. The best way to do this on an outback tour is to go bush camping. With the sun low and the cockatiels bursting from the trees, we'd go plunketing down some dirt track. Occasionally I'd play songs from *The Lion King* because, for some reason, hearing an African-themed soundtrack while bouncing through the Australian bush made people feel more at home.

When we stopped in a clearing and turned off the engine, sometimes there'd be confusion.

'But there is *nothing*.'

'I know! Isn't it wonderful?'

Bush camping worked for many reasons, chief among them that no one wants to die alone. The tourists would come out of the bus in small groups and look around. It was like a small-time survival camp. Strangers would go off to pee together and come back friends, or scatter in twos and threes to collect firewood, and get bitten by ants. I watched it all proudly from the top of the trailer.

There'd be some incredulous German guy saying, 'Don't you have a chainsaw? For making the firewood? Or some axes?'

We didn't, of course, but they always worked it out. Sometimes I hid the matches, to make it even more fun for them.

Those were always the best nights, with no one around and the Milky Way smeared across the black sky. We drank beer and cooked paella with chicken and chorizo next to the fire.

People really started talking, and slept closer to one another than on any other nights.

There are other ways of getting a group together, of course. I know a guide who, if he sensed malaise, would fake a flat battery and make everyone get out and push-start the bus. That's good as gold, as far as bonding goes. So is getting bogged and digging the bus out with salad bowls. I once tried to fix a radiator leak with Blu-Tack, but didn't have any Blu-Tack, so I passed around packets of chewing gum. If you can get twenty-one people all chewing gum for a common cause, what you have is a family.

Most tourists book the tour to see Uluru, but it's the experiences in between that really make the trip memorable. Your job is to provide the context in which a tourist can enjoy or appreciate them. Take Coober Pedy, for instance. Some guides treat it with disdain, or like an overrated lunch spot – and their tourists inevitably go away feeling the same way.

The town itself is built on a hot and sandy moonscape. It looks like a dusty Hobbiton, an 'after' shot in a film about global warming. The first thing you see when you're coming into Coober Pedy from the south is a lone wind turbine resolutely not turning.

It looks a bit like a dump, frankly, but I'm inordinately fond of it, and that's contagious. Most of the front yards have assorted junk piles that take on a majestic rusted glow at sunset. People have built themselves terraced front yards from old car tyres. There is half a spaceship on the main street, and a tree that appears to be made from scrap metal. The early miners built the tree for their kids, apparently, who complained constantly about not having any decent trees to climb. Even when it was built, though, they could only climb it during a few months of every year without getting second-degree burns on their hands and feet.

I always liked to take my tours to the Coober Pedy Opal Fields Golf Course. Sometimes it's hard to find the golf balls among all the similarly sized rocks. The rest is baked clay and sand, and the players have to carry around their own patch of turf to play the balls off. But it's the only golf course in the world to have a reciprocal membership arrangement with the world-famous St Andrews Links in Scotland. There's a sign by the sixth hole that says 'Keep Off Grass', which sums up the whole town nicely, I think.

From Coober Pedy to Uluru-Kata Tjuta National Park it's about seven hundred kilometres – not a lot by Australian standards, but enough of a drive to demoralise you and the tourists. Try to surround yourself with good people up the front of the bus. If it doesn't happen by chance on the first day, suggest that swapping seats every morning is a great thing to do. Drink coffee and eat apples like a fiend to stay awake, tell stories over the microphone and play games.

There are signs up and down that highway with sage, big-lettered messages like 'POWERNAP NOW' or 'FEELING SLEEPY?' Those signs will make you indescribably angry. You have to try not to think about sleep at all, but those thoughts can sneak up on you: you check in your mirror to make sure the swags are still tied down, you start thinking about your own swag and how comfortable it is, and suddenly you feel your eyelids drooping. Try to think only of very active things, like being chased by wolves or robbing a supermarket.

On the way to Uluru, there's a flat-top mesa mountain called Mount Conner. This kind of mountain is a much more common formation, geologically speaking, than Uluru, which is why Uluru has its own airport and Mt Conner has two toilets and a barbecue. But Mount Conner stands majestically by itself on the desert plain, so it's often mistaken for Ayers Rock. (Locals call it 'Fool-a-roo'.)

Everyone gets excited and goes reaching for their cameras because it's a good-looking mountain. One time, when we were stopped in the car park and I explained how it wasn't actually Uluru, I saw a Swiss couple put away their camera without even taking the photo. I was outraged. 'Guys, *it's the same mountain*! It's the same mountain it was thirty seconds ago when you were all in a tizzy about it!'

But people want the rock they paid for. You can't just go springing a mountain on people and expecting them to fall in love with it.

The last hour before sundown is a beautiful time in the outback, Uluru or no. A sudden aching softness comes to a landscape that just five minutes ago seemed barren and unrelenting. I always felt beers were important at a time like that, because you wanted everyone to slow down for what was going on. You could tell the non-drinkers, because they were impatient for something to happen. (Like, what? Uluru miraculously spewing lava?)

Sometimes, if I felt the whole thing could benefit from a sense of occasion, I would tell them that this was the very sand dune from which William Gosse (a white dude) and his party first laid eyes on Uluru. People really liked that. They *oohed*.

'But couldn't they have seen it from the sand dune just over there?'

There's always one.

'You raise a good point, madam.'

I never had qualms about butchering the European version of things. For one thing, most of the best places are just named after some dude. What are you going to do, stand in front of that beautiful rock with its thirty thousand-year-old cultural history and talk about So-and-so Ayers who once governed South Australia and had certain hobbies?

One should never let facts get in the way of a good story, because no one remembers facts anyway. The best tour guides will turn an explanation into a story that's entertaining, even to someone who cares nothing for the subject matter.

Then you'd hear the spiels of other guides: 'Now, the canyon is made up of two types of sandstone: the Mereenie sandstone, which is 400 million years old, and the Carmichael sandstone, which is 360 million years old …'

If there was ever a more boring sentence in the English language, I didn't finish reading it. No one's heard of the Mereenie or the Carmichael sandstone. Furthermore, no one can properly imagine how old 400 million years is, *or*, for that matter, 360 million years. What exactly are the tourists being offered that they can't get themselves with an encyclopaedia and a tranquilliser dart?

You have to start early in the mornings. If you let the tourists sleep in and start the walks too late in the day, it will take them a whole day to recover from the heat. The desert is alive in the early mornings, more alive than most can imagine. As the morning goes on, the shadows shorten and the sun drains the colour from the trees. Eleven am brings the death of hope. There's no more birdsong, just the sounds of buzzing flies and sobbing. You explain this to your passengers well in advance; you want them to feel like they have made the choice (though there is no choice), so they feel like mavericks in the early morning, and not like they've been bullied into it.

The other thing we did in the summertime was sneak people into the five-star hotel pool. It was beautiful: shady trees, deckchairs and waiters delivering poolside cocktails – luxuries like that are wasted on the rich. I used to explain the layout of the place to my crew and arm everyone with elaborate backstories to explain how such a ragtag bunch had come into enough money to afford a five-star hotel. Then I would drop them off in groups of twos and threes at various locations and staggered intervals. I'm not sure any of this was entirely necessary, but it helped with the sense of occasion.

The Australian tourism industry is overrun with white bread and overcooked sausages. If you learn to cook healthily for twenty-one people, with a bit of panache and without it looking like a bucket of slops, you will go a long way. You can use economies of scale to provide much better meals than they could ever manage on their own.

It almost (*almost*) doesn't matter what you show them during the day, if you feed them well at night. I always carried a packet of Tim Tams with me for when things got rough, the way a cop sleeps with a gun under his pillow.

German girls will commit heinous crimes for Nutella at breakfast time. Europeans in general will not eat white bread, and you shouldn't bother making them try. The smallest girls from Taiwan and Korea will eat twice as much as any man. And although some Italian men might be incapable of opening a tin of tomatoes, they will nevertheless have strong and vocal opinions on how to make the bolognaise. These should largely be ignored.

On the last night of our tour, we would cook up a big gourmet barbecue at Uluru and have a candlelit dinner. Once everything was ready to go I would hit the lights, plunging us into a darkness broken only by the flickering of candles, and then play Marvin Gaye.

The real difficulty on those nights was not the cooking of the dinner, but the getting people to eat it. They all wanted to take photos of it: sometimes there'd be so many people jostling at the end of the table that there was no one left to photograph. Just me, sitting there like a schmuck, and a sixty-year-old Frenchwoman saying, 'I never did understand Facebook.'

The catering should never *look* difficult. Some of my worst tour incidents were precipitated by struggles with over-extravagant (and complicated) meals. I still cringe to think about the night I wrapped quails in sage and prosciutto, and spent two hours trying to balance them over hot coals in a pot-belly stove. The problem was this: no one wants to see their guide running around like a desperate MasterChef contestant. It's unbecoming.

There is a subtle but important difference between taking care of your passengers and *serving* them. When they see you running around like I did with the quails, it feels like servitude. And in gaining a servant, they lose a leader. It can spoil a group. You're taking on expectations that can never be met, and they will resent you for it in ways they don't entirely understand. They will start blaming you for the flies, the weather, the mediocre sunsets.

Two days after the quail incident, I was still feeling the shame of a bad parent. And then, forty kilometres out of Glendambo, I started smelling burning oil. It had already been a trip filled with mechanical problems: we'd blown a heater hose and had to swap buses; we'd had flat tyres and an air-conditioning system that wheezed like an emphysema patient trying to get out his last words. Our exhaust had broken in two places and was held together with an olive oil tin. I was just trying to keep it all together. When I smelled the oil I almost didn't stop – by this stage the tourists and I were engaged in high-level psychological warfare, and I didn't want to lose any more ground – but it smelled like the end of days.

I got out and trudged down the back. The whole underside of

the bus and the front of the trailer were sprayed in oil. I opened the engine block and it was absolute carnage; it looked like a Tarantino movie in black and white. But I could see exactly where the oil had come from: a big round hole that should have had a cap screwed over it. I knew this because I'd taken it off the night before to top up the oil. And now we'd lost all of it through the same hole. By some miracle, the cap was still sitting there upside down right where I'd left it. I dropped the cover on the engine block and cleared my throat.

The tourists looked at me with deep suspicion.

'Folks,' I said, 'we've got ourselves an oil leak.' (Which was technically true.) 'In the gasket region.' (Which was not.)

There were outraged groans. Someone threw his St Christopher medal out the window.

'Now listen,' I said, holding up my hands, 'I'm pretty sure I can fix the leak.'

I *was* sure I could fix the leak, insofar as screwing the cap back on would pretty much do the trick, but there was still the problem of the oil.

We had just enough left to make it to Glendambo. While everyone was preparing lunch, I topped it up and told them I was off to fix the leak. I parked the bus behind the roadhouse and sat there drinking a Gatorade and reading *Moby-Dick*. I called my mechanic friend in Adelaide and asked her if she knew enough about gaskets to explain to me how I might pretend to have fixed one. Then I tastefully applied some engine grease to my face so it'd look like I'd been busy, and drove back around to the lunch spot. I was beeping the horn and hanging out the window: 'Guys, I fucking *fixed* it!' And it really felt like I had. On some tours you will claim any victory you can in order to get you home.

When you get a bad group, whether it's your fault or theirs, the first day or two can be funny. It can be entertaining to see the lengths some people will go to just to have a terrible time. But by the third day you can't remember who your friends are or if you even have any. You go looking for love wherever you can find it.

The girls who like you will often watch you in the rear-view mirror while you're driving. Sometimes they're wearing sunglasses, which makes it hard to tell. I know a guide who, if he wanted to find out, would yawn deliberately into the rear-view mirror. He could tell by people's psychosomatic responses (aka yawning back) who was watching from behind their sunglasses.

I tried the yawning thing once, but concerned passengers kept coming up to the front of the bus and suggesting we do singalongs or asking me if I wanted to stop for coffee. The gibber plains stretched out interminably.

'*Where?*' I said. 'Where would we stop?'

I can speak fluent German. I thought it would be a secret weapon, which I could use for good if I wanted to or evil if I needed to. In six years of tour guiding, I almost never eavesdropped on anything interesting.

At Uluru sunsets there was a lot of '*Ja*, I have been thinking the same thing! Why does he cut the tomatoes so thick at lunchtime? Sometimes they are thicker than the bread even!' What sounds like complaining is really just Germans having a good time. They love bonding over logistical mishaps. It can really kill a good story, though, because they're always laughing at the wrong bit. You start off setting the scene, explaining how you were in Sydney this one time, and you were caught in the rain because the bus was late, and suddenly the Germans are all falling about with laughter. 'I know, I know!' they say, with tears streaming down their faces. 'The buses are *always* late!'

At Uluru I was doing some paperwork outside the cultural centre's gift shop. It was late afternoon but hot still, and the flies were getting their second wind. I was sipping a cold lemonade.

A German girl had been giving me grief for five days straight. Some people are just hard to live with. She plonked herself down across the table from me and started staring at my drink. Her friend sat down too.

Without taking her eyes off my drink, the girl said to her friend, in German, 'Look at that *drink*.' Then she let out a little moan. 'Ooooooh, what would you give for a drink like that? I'd give *anything* for a drink like that.'

I was genuinely confused: *They're $3.50 in the same gift shop you just came out of. You don't have to give* anything.

Her moaning was making me uncomfortable, on account of its rising pitch.

I said, 'Listen, would you like the rest of my lemonade?'

She looked at me suddenly with wide eyes and clutched the drink with both hands. 'No, I couldn't. I shouldn't. Maybe I could ...? Can I?'

Then, as she brought it to her mouth, she turned to her friend and said, in her native tongue, 'Wait. Do you think he's diseased?'

Something broke inside me that day. I jumped up and started screaming at her in German. I mentioned unmentionable things. I said, 'Holy Christ, after everything I've done for you today, after all the things, the sneaking you into the five-star pool at great personal risk etc. now this?!'

She was pleasantly surprised.

'Oh! Why didn't you tell us? You're German! That's why you have such good ideas, like the pool!'

Usually I wouldn't let on until the fifth or sixth day, when we'd just got back from hiking, and people were hot and exhausted and thinking of other things. I would plug the microphone in and just start giving the spiel in German.

On the last morning we'd hike Kings Canyon together. The group would climb to the top of 'Heart Attack Hill', essentially the final summit. They'd look back across the desert plains and feel – justifiably so, in some respects – that they had survived the outback. And they'd feel like they did it together. A long-distance tour is so different from a day tour. The group takes on a character all of its own, and has its own hand in shaping the trip's narrative. Four hours later, we'd traipse out of the canyon, and though they wouldn't all be friends, even the villains and the sullen damsels would have played their part.

It's only five hours from Kings Canyon to Alice Springs, but it was going to be a tough drive: we'd had a 5am start and hiked four hours in the heat. I got everyone going with the coffee and the French toast, which the French couple insisted was just toast, then snuck off into the bushes for a power nap. I told the group we'd pack up camp and hit the road by 11.30.

Next thing I knew I woke up groggy and confused to the sound of the bus horn. Somehow it was 11.30 already and I'd missed everything. I jumped up and ran back to camp. I was irritated that they were beeping the horn instead of doing anything useful. When I got outside I saw that they were all just sitting there on the bus. 'For the love of God, *guys*,' I started to yell, 'we've got to pack this place *up*!'

And then I saw the swags tied down on the roof. I walked into our hut and everything was gone. The food boxes, the bags, the cooking equipment had all been packed into the trailer; the place was swept up and wiped down. It had never looked so good. They'd even scrubbed out the fridge. The only thing left in the place was a cup of fresh coffee with my name on it. They were beeping the horn because everything was done. It was taken care of, and all they needed was me.

Originally published in The Monthly, *June 2015*

FELICITY WARD

10 Reasons Mary Poppins is a Jerk

If you take the sound away, the film is pretty much ninety minutes of Mary Poppins rolling her eyes. I'm surprised she didn't pull an optic nerve.

I get it: *Mary Poppins* is a beloved children's film. It's what warm fuzzies are made of. But after a 'movie night at Aunty Flick's house' I realised, in front of my adoring niece, that there was something harrowing about this film: Mary Poppins is a total jerk.

Now, before you rush to the defence of everyone's favourite rose-cheeked, Super(califragilisticexpialidocious) Nanny, let me tell you what I'm on about.

1. Her judgy-ness

The title of this movie could easily be changed to *Mary Poppins and What She Thinks of Your Stupid Face*. Mary must be a banker, because she keeps putting her two cents in about how everyone would be better off if they were just more like her. If you take the sound away, the film is pretty much ninety minutes of Mary Poppins rolling her eyes. I'm surprised she didn't pull an optic nerve.

> Scene from (my) Director's Cut:
> *Mary is groaning, bent down, cupping a hand over one eye.*
> *Young child, Michael, enters, concerned.*
> MICHAEL: What's wrong, Mary Poppins?

Mary, pointing at her eye socket.

MARY: Awww ... owww ... I was just better than everyone.

Fin.

I get the same feeling watching Morgan Freeman. Don't get me wrong, the man can act. But in every role, he has that same *I-don't-want-to-say-I-told-you-so* smile, and I'm like, 'Yes you do, Morgan Freeman. That's all you want to say.'

Unlike Morgan, Mary loves pointing it out. If it's not their outfit, it's their tardiness. If it's not their tardiness, it's that they're a two-dimensional animated character singing a song about a horserace. Nothing is ever enough.

Within the first five minutes of getting what is obviously a much sought-after au pair job, she looks around her new bedroom and snarks, 'Well, it's not exactly Buckingham Palace.' No, Mez, it's not. And I don't think the Queen advertises for nannies through the *Trading Post*, or on handwritten letters penned by barely literate children.

If those two kids, Jane and Michael, weren't as dumb as two stones, I'd be worried her mentorship was doing long-term damage. Fortunately they rarely have a thought between them for the duration of the film.

2. Her martyr complex, and the poor sods she takes it out on

He's a street artist, he's a chimney sweep, he's a one-man band. He is: Dick Van Dyke. Despite the many jobs he holds (which most parents would call a 'red flag'), he has a heart of gold and a tooth of coal. All he wants to do is show Mary and the kids that he can take them on a magical adventure to another dimension. Wide eyes, big dreams, Bert.

Now we can all agree that transcending the space-time continuum is a difficult thing for anyone to pull off, yeah? I'd say ... harder than folding a fitted sheet; not as hard as trying to understand why anyone would go on that show *Embarrassing Bodies*. (They could have a sore elbow but we'll still somehow end up seeing their anus!)

But Dick Van Dyke tries his best anyway, because he wants these dear people to have a day out to remember. He doesn't succeed, bless his cotton socks, but at least he tried ... right? Right, Mary? He tried? It's the trying that counts, isn't it?

Nope. Enter Martyr Poppins, and she is not impressed. She waltzes in, grabs Dick's hand. Grabs the kids' hands. Sighs. 'Why do you always complicate things that are really quite simple?' (Um, JERK ALERT.) Shoots him a look that says, 'I am too old for this shit', and performs what can only be described as the most resentful magic trick of all time.

Well good on you, Mary. Not everyone is a natural Time Lord, you know? The only thing Dick Van Dyke owns that travels well is his accent; it's like a cockney vinyl record left to melt in the sun. Even watching it now, I can barely make out a word he says. If only you could get frequent flyer points for an accent. He'd be a platinum member by now, able to fly himself away from Mary Poppins.

Does it feel good being better than a chimney sweep, Mary? A chimney sweep whose name is Dick Van Dyke?! He literally has the words 'penis' and 'lesbian' in his name. Don't kick a man while he's down. That's probably why he's a chimney sweep: he got bullied at school, then had to leave when he was ten. Even if we call him by his initials it's still insultingly prophetic, as anything Dick Van Dyke made after *Diagnosis: Murder* probably went straight to DVD.

3. The song 'A Spoonful of Sugar'

By 2025, it is estimated that five million people in the UK will have diabetes. Get current, Mez. Kids are dying.

4. She's a liar

It's pretty clear that Mary is a witch. She flies in on a talking umbrella. She slides *up* the banister to the children's room. She has a magical carpetbag. Let's be real about this. Broom = umbrella. It's a matter of accessories. They were well and truly out of the 'witch-burning years' in 1910, so why not come clean with it? Because Mary Poppins is a liar. Or maybe she's just deluded. 'I am kind but extremely firm.' Well, she's half right. I've slept on concrete softer than Mary Poppins.

5. The carpetbag of bottomless disappointment

Okay, picture this: you have a bag that can travel anywhere in the world with you. You can put whatever you want into it, and it will never get full. What do you take?! A Shetland pony? The cast of Cirque du Soleil? A fully-functioning TARDIS? No. Mary Poppins, the most boring woman in the world, brings a hatstand, lamp, mirror, hand mirror, measuring tape and an interior plant. What a party animal. Never trust a woman who wants to get down with a ficus. More so, one who travels with a full-length mirror *and* a hand mirror? No one even MENTIONS the fact that she packed them without bubble wrap. That's pathological! But Mary's mirror obsession makes total sense because ...

6. Mary is a certified narcissist

Getting ready to leave the house, Mary stops to check herself out in the mirror (a house mirror, not her travel mirror, or her hand mirror – *ugh*).

I mean it *is* her favourite view. Why wouldn't she get one more eyeful of Chez Mez before she has to gaze upon those dreary twerps she's contractually obliged to entertain? So, there she is, just singing along merrily (Mary-ly?) to herself and giving spoonfuls of sugar a bad name, when her reflection takes on a life of its own and starts to sing out a call and response, as if she's some sort of operatic Fatman Scoop. ('*If you got short hair make nooooise!*') Mary is delighted that her mirrored self has joined in on an afternoon harmony ... and why not? That's one more Poppins in the world. She's already had a warble with a sparrow, so why not croon along with her own haunted reflection? (She will literally do anything to avoid having to engage with those kids.)

But what happens when you encourage even the shadow of an egomaniac? Like Gremlins fed after midnight, they get out of control. So it's all well and good that Mez is ready to walk off and leave, but her shadow-self stops her dead by breaking out into a 100 per cent unnecessary vocal solo. It ain't over till the hat lady sings. You created this monster, Mary-ah Carey – you deal with it.

7. Hypocrisy, thy name is Poppins

After showing the children how to clean up via the miracle of percussion, then having a duet with herself in the mirror, Mary turns around and gives the kids a bit of 'don't be all day about it, please'.

I'm pretty sure you're the one holding up proceedings, ding-dong, not the six- and eight-year-olds who just want to love you.

That's the great thing about Mary having magical powers: she can move the goalposts whenever she likes. Nearly every bit of advice Mary dishes out is contradicted minutes later. Take this sentence:

'Never judge things by their appearance. I'm sure I never do.'

Then a scene or two later she's pulling this shit out:

'Let me look at you. Well, you're not as turned-out as I'd like.'

This from a woman who's wearing a hat covered in plastic flowers, indoors! It's England, babes, you don't need a hat anywhere.

8. Everyone loves to laugh. Except Mary.

I tell you what, for someone so universally cherished, Mary Poppins sure does hate having a good time. The problem is, *she* thinks she's a hessian sack of fun. Here's Mary responding to the children's wish list for a better class of nanny:

'Item one: a cheery disposition. [Pause] I am never cross.'

I don't know if Mary understands words. The absence of anger is not the presence of glee. That's like being asked, 'Do you love animals?' and responding with, 'I've never drowned one.'

And the Sheriff of Frown Town represents the badge at every turn. At one point in the film, Mary receives an important phone call. By which I mean a dog named Andrew barks a message at her (Andrew: classic dog name), and she completely understands. Of course she speaks dog. Apparently Uncle Albert (never been mentioned before, still don't know who he is) is in a terrible state, and when they arrive at his house he's literally flying around his ceiling in fits of hysterical laughter. What seems to be the problem? That the old man is enjoying himself. Sure, he's levitating, but nobody seems particularly bothered with that. Hey, guys, last time I checked, PEOPLE DON'T FLY!

Like any serious disease, Uncle Albert's laughter becomes infectious, and the next thing you know, Bert, Jane and Michael are caught giggling up in the air. As you can imagine, Mary is steaming at the carpetbag about this (see previous self-analysis: 'I am never cross.' LIAAAAAAR). Maybe she was worried someone would actually piss themselves with laughter and she'd be stuck, staring from the ground ...

9. The endless mind games

At the end of the film, she denies any of the madness ever happened. This is called gaslighting, Mary, and it's a technique used by bullies to make others feel insecure and crazy. It's undermining and abusive. *Put that on your CV, dipshit!* 'MARY POPPINS: NOT SAFE FOR CHILDREN!'

10. That scene where she measures the height of the children

Even by this stage in the film, it is clear that Jane and Michael have succumbed to Stockholm syndrome and are desperately in love with their captor. Mary Poppins rushes through their tape measurements, both children getting something to the effect of 'your father never loved you'. (Historically, Mr Banks was a neglectful father, so I'm not far off.) Then Mary gets to the grand prize that she's been waiting for: herself. She looks at the tape measure, acts faux-embarrassed, but then still somehow musters up the courage to read out her findings:

'Practically perfect in every way.'

You know what, Mary Poppins? If you're so perfect how come you're in your thirties and you're still babysitting?

And there you have it. A beat-by-beat breakdown of why Mary Poppins, beloved nanny, is actually a bona fide arsehole. Next movie night, my niece deserves something better, more uplifting ... maybe that lovely *Nemo* film. You know, the one about the dead mother and the abandoned son ... or maybe *Beauty and the Beast*, where the woman is held hostage until she learns to love her kidnapper ... You know what, maybe I'll just teach my three-year-old niece how to knife fight? Might be less damaging.

BEN POBJIE

Diary of a Respected Actor

‘Before I left Spielberg's office, he whispered in my ear, 'I hate movies. I always have.' Didn't know what to say.’

September 18

Lunched with Martin Scorsese and Thelma Schoonmaker. Scorsese seemed distracted, continually batting away imaginary moths. Thelma had to tell him several times to stop sniffing his veal. They told me they had a great role for me in their next movie. They want me to play a sassy mummy in the NYPD. Am not sure about this; don't want to get typecast.

September 21

Spent all day reading scripts. One in particular caught my eye, a Civil War story. Very good dialogue, only problem is script is only six pages long and has no characters. Might need polishing. Called Akiva Goldsman and left message with his personal slave asking Akiva to call back.

September 22

Akiva called back but insisted on speaking to me in Russian, and the conversation went nowhere. Dropped round to Bill Goldman's place, but he tried to shoot me. Have decided to polish script myself. Main thing is to introduce protagonist early and develop the themes of familial loss and ingrained prejudice. Also, change setting from 1950s Egypt to 1863 Virginia in order to make the Civil War themes more authentic.

September 24

Today I went to the theatre. Wandered around for a while, but was unable to find the door. Went home again. Cried. Cut myself. Felt better. It reminded me of my old days at NIDA, when we would rehearse all day and then go drinking all night, and completely forget to go to the theatre to perform the play. I was there eight years and never once got onto a stage. I used to feel bad about this, but a few months back I ran into Hugh Jackman, and he told me he'd never been on a stage either – he uses a system of mirrors to project an image of himself. 'I do all my acting in a van outside the theatre,' he chuckled. Later he made me promise not to reveal that he is still alive.

September 30

Woke up with renewed energy. Tomorrow is the start of principal photography on *Hammer of Love*. Am extremely excited about this film. Feel I may be a chance for an Oscar. Hilda disagrees, says the story makes no sense, but I think if I play it with subtle nuance I can make it work. Am slightly concerned that the real MC Hammer may not like my portrayal.

October 1

First day of shooting was a disaster. Began with climactic harpoon battle atop Taj Mahal scene. First shot of the day, the cameraman exploded. We lost half a day getting new cameraman, and then Jennifer Lawrence wouldn't come out of her trailer. She said the

Cobra Queen costume makes her look fat. I agreed, loudly, and was scolded for being unhelpful. Retired to my own trailer to sulk and read *Dianetics*. There's a lot of good common sense in there. Called my agent, demanded a box of insulin. She told me I'd misunderstood the book. Fired her on the spot.

October 4

We have solved the problem of the ambiguous ending. Now, instead of Hammer taking Wendy for a helicopter ride over Florence, he shoots her. Racial tension is thereby much more effectively conveyed. The different ending was my idea. Am very proud of myself. In the evening did more work on Civil War script. Have decided to make main character gay and Finnish. Was unsure of whether to go through with this change, but Albert Finney told me to 'trust my instincts'. Must see more of Albert; he always cheers me up, and has some high-grade heroin.

October 8

Jennifer is a nightmare to work with. She insists on carrying her Golden Globes around at all times in huge saddlebags attached to her hips, including when on camera. She tells the director to 'edit them out with CGI'. She has also made a unilateral decision to give the Cobra Queen a severe lisp. I no longer have any idea what she is saying in our scenes together and have to improvise. Was told off in embassy ball scene for improvising kicking Jennifer in the neck. Sulked for an hour, then felt bad and apologised to entire cast and crew and took them out for pancakes. Jennifer ate seventeen pancakes by herself, then burped on everyone. The woman is a disgrace.

October 15

Location shooting in Scotland for several days, doubling for Morocco. I will be glad when this film is finished. It has taken a lot out of me. My own script is progressing well, and is practically writing itself since I put in the speedboat chase. Today is Jennifer's last day on set, and we will all be thankful when she is gone. Her bad behaviour caused the complete abandonment of the Nazi spy subplot, and the movie is now more focused on the love triangle between Hammer, Wendy and Joan Jett. Jennifer has insisted on a best boy credit. I think this is a mistake. Tried to kill her in Scotland, but the gunpowder got wet.

October 16

Last night made love to Jennifer over and over again. The greatest night of my life. In the morning she was gone, leaving only a note scrawled in lipstick on my foot: 'BEWARE'. This is typical.

October 23

Finished shoot for *Hammer of Love* with animatronic dinosaur scene. Director decided movie would be funnier if MC Hammer starts out as white but has to pretend to be black to avoid Mafia. See his point, but was unaware movie was a comedy. Huge wrap party held at the Governor's Mansion, without the Governor's knowledge, so we had to be extremely quiet. Were almost discovered when Maggie Gyllenhaal vomited in the dining room, but the Governor blamed his dog. Much fun had by all. Also finished the Civil War script, which is now over eight hundred pages long and in Hebrew. Extremely pleased with it.

October 24

Woke up feeling bloated. Called my rabbi to ask whether I should try paleo. He told me he wasn't my rabbi. Feel strange.

October 26

Emailed Joan Allen to find out whether she wanted to go out with me. She emailed back saying yes. Then on IMDB, found out that I had actually wanted to ask Jane Lynch. Very embarrassed. Emailed Joan Allen again to say I had a bad head cold. Turns out she finds this very sexy. There is no way out!

October 31

Went to Kevin Smith's Halloween party, as usual. My costume (Cary Elwes in *Twister*) was a huge success. Ended the night on back of a flatbed truck with Bradley Cooper while he listed all of the football games he's ever seen. Just before he got off the truck, Bradley gave me a large baby. 'I think he's better off with you,' he said, and leaped into the darkness.

November 2

Bumped into Reese Witherspoon at McDonald's. She's looking well. She was most agitated about the insufficient number of napkins she had been given. Showed her the napkin dispenser, for which she declared herself 'eternally grateful'. She said she would love to star in my Civil War movie, as the avaricious pearl diver. I asked did she know anything about pearls? Reese said she didn't, but she had an uncle who bred ostriches, which were 'kind of the same'. I cannot help but admire her optimism.

November 3

Phone call from Dustin Hoffman, complaining about my negative review of *Tootsie* in the *LA Times*. Explained to him that *Tootsie* came out in 1982 and I am not a critic, and he apologised very graciously. Explained he had become a little scatterbrained since being run over by Renee Zellweger. Said I knew the feeling. We reminisced about the time we jumped Tobey Maguire outside Grauman's and spent the night making him kiss tramps at gunpoint. Dustin asked if he could play General Lee in the Civil War film – I said he'd be perfect, but I would have to figure out a way to get Kathy Bates fired first. He suggested spreading a rumour that she is a Muslim. I said I'd think about it. He made disturbing kissy noises down the phone before hanging up. I wonder if he's alright.

November 5

Met with Harvey Weinstein to secure financing for Civil War script, which now has the working title *Suck My Dixie*. He said he'd stump up six billion of his own money, as long as he could have final approval on grip selection. He also suggested Azealia Banks to direct 'to give it that old-world art deco feel'. Didn't say anything as I didn't want to risk the six billion. He asked me for a lift home as his car was in rehab. I was happy to oblige, obviously.

November 6

Rang Harvey Weinstein's office to go over detail on contract. Weinstein remembered nothing of our meeting. After some confusing conversations, discovered I actually spoke to Harvey Fierstein, who has been in a hospital for the criminally insane for three years. Regretting giving him that lift.

November 7

Police came to house asking about Fierstein. I told them I had never heard of him. They told me confidentially that they weren't actually police officers, but escaped murderers. I lauded their initiative and gave them a drink. While we were celebrating, real policemen showed up. We all had a good laugh. I am now under arrest for the kidnap and murder of Harvey Fierstein.

November 8

Lawyer convinced judge to drop kidnapping charge in exchange for a role in my next movie. Thought this was a good deal, but it turned out the agreement specifies the judge must play a giant super-intelligent shark. Could be a problem in the Civil War setting. But I can't go to jail – the last time I was in there, I was the target of several hurtful remarks.

November 9

Spent all day in meetings with Spielberg, trying to convince him to direct the Civil War film, now provisionally titled *The Shark Who Burnt Atlanta*. He finally agreed, but insisted that John Williams compose the score and George Lucas provide catering services. This seems reasonable. Before I left Spielberg's office, he whispered in my ear, 'I hate movies. I always have.' Didn't know what to say.

November 10

There are sixty-one messages on my phone from Spielberg, all begging me to save him from the deadly illusions that plague his soul. Slightly embarrassing.

November 11

Did not get a wink of sleep. Spielberg spent whole night throwing pebbles at my window and screaming, 'Release me from my celluloid prison, put an end to the imaginary picture-people who wish to kill me.' Especially awkward as I was in bed with Emma Stone. She told me not to worry because it happens to all men, but I doubt this, to be honest.

November 12

Received a telegram asking for my advice on the development of new, all-female Ghostbusters film. Quite delighted to find that the rumours about Paul Feig communicating only via telegram are true. Now in a dilemma: would be a dream to work on Ghostbusters, but telegram strongly implies that Paul wants my advice because he believes me to be a ghost. Should I disabuse him and risk losing the opportunity? Headed next door to ask Sally Field what she thought, but she was in one of her moods and stabbed me in the neck quite hard. Definitely one of those days I'm glad I divorced her.

November 17

BuzzFeed is reporting that Russell Crowe and I are father and son, but you have to take out a paid subscription to find out which of us is which. On principle I don't pay for news, but I confess I am curious. Had lunch with Russell: he's not sure either.

November 28

Heard there is a lot of Oscar buzz around my performance in *Hammer of Love*. Not surprised, I was fantastic. Also heard that Jennifer has threatened to blow up a hospital for every award I win. I guess the

Academy voters will decide whose side they're on. The publicity can only help *The Shark Who Burnt Atlanta*, although the studio is now saying they prefer the title *Gettysburg Car Wash 8*. I am willing to compromise.

December 8

Have had a wonderful idea and rewritten my script. It is still set during the Civil War, but now focuses on a sarcastic family of werewolves on the run from werewolf hunters hiding out in a convent. Title is now *Creatures of Habit*. Emailed Hugh Grant to tell him about it. Hugh emailed back, saying it was a wonderful idea, but plot should also involve backgammon in some way. Lately Hugh has been obsessed with backgammon, and it becomes tiresome. He has four movies lined up, all backgammon-themed. The irony is, he doesn't even know how to play backgammon. Agreed to meet him for lunch tomorrow, as we have not seen each other in a while.

December 9

Lunch with Hugh was a little embarrassing. Continually had to slap his hand away from my thigh. He told me he suspected Joe Pesci of stealing his food. Would normally dismiss this, but Pesci has form; several years ago he stole all the maps out of my glove compartment. Macaulay Culkin told me that on the set of *Home Alone* everybody was instructed to keep their valuables on high shelves. Hugh confided in me that he has fallen in love with Thandie Newton, but does not know how to express his feelings. I advised him to be honest and direct, and he collapsed in tears. Most embarrassing. I had to ring Rachel Weisz and ask her to come pick him up. Amazing woman, she has the strength of an ox.

December 11

Had a great idea for *Creatures of Habit*: I intend to play both the head werewolf AND the Mother Superior. Emailed Eddie Murphy for advice on prosthetics. No reply yet. Call from Jeffrey Katzenberg, who says the movie can be about werewolves, but dislikes the name *Creatures of Habit*: He prefers *The Adventures of Brian Dennehy, Rocketeer*. Katzenberg also thinks the entire thing needs to be filmed on location in Vanuatu. I am not averse to any of these suggestions, but it does seem a bit presumptuous of him, given he is not attached to the film in any way.

December 12

Eddie Murphy emailed back to say I could borrow his fat suit, but only if I drove him to the airport. Emailed him back to say no deal.

December 13

Eddie turned up on my doorstep with suitcases. Angrily told him I was definitely not driving him to airport. Eddie started to cry and told me he never learned to read. Agreed to drive him to airport. On the way, he insisted on doing terrible Lily Allen impressions the whole time. When we got to the airport, he tried to convince me to come with him, hidden in his luggage. Said I was far too busy. He started to cry again. Beat a hasty retreat.

December 14

News this morning says Eddie Murphy has hijacked an American Airlines flight and redirected it to Chad. Must confess, am surprised.

December 15

Eddie called me, explaining he meant to direct them to Chad Lowe. He had assumed everyone knew what he meant, but now he is very hot and a camel spat on him. He asked me to wire him some money. Explained I don't actually know what that means. Hung up while he was crying.

December 16

Fantastic day! Call from Pixar saying they are putting my script into production with Paul Reiser as the voice of Ulysses Grant, Tina Fey as Lincoln, and Seth Rogen as Grandpa Werewolf. They will rewrite my script to remove all references to chemtrails and *The Protocols of Zion*, and the final title is *Walter the Talking Nectarine*: but I do get Randy Newman approval. Also heard from Ron Howard, who wants me to play ALF in his sequel to *Apollo 13*. Finally my career seems to be on the move. Celebrated long into the night with champagne and air hockey games with Brett Ratner. As I fell asleep in Emma's arms, heard a distant explosion. Can't wait to find out what I've won!

NOTES ON CONTRIBUTORS

James Colley is a Young Walkley-nominated satirist, founder of SBS Comedy's The Backburner, writer for *The Weekly* with Charlie Pickering, researcher for *Gruen*, comedy producer on FBi's *Backchat*, creator of 2SER's *Stop the Posts*, writer for *A Rational Fear* and all-round idiot for hire.

Annabel Crabb is one of Australia's most popular political commentators, a Walkley-awarded writer, and the host of Australia's first dedicated political cooking show, ABC TV's *Kitchen Cabinet*. She writes for ABC Online's *The Drum* and has worked extensively in TV and radio. She is a columnist for the *Sunday Age*, *Sun-Herald* and Canberra's *Sunday Times*, and has worked as a political correspondent and sketchwriter for titles including the *Advertiser*, the *Age* and the *Sydney Morning Herald*, and as London correspondent for Fairfax's Sunday papers. She won a Walkley Award for her 2009 essay on Malcolm Turnbull, and was Australia's 2011 Eisenhower Fellow. Annabel is an enthusiastic social media user and tweets about politics and food as @annabelcrabb. She lives in Sydney with her partner, Jeremy, and their three children.

Andrew Denton has worked extensively in every medium except crayon. He describes himself as 'too pretty for television and too ugly for radio', and on visa forms lists his occupation as 'personality'. He counts Rupert Murdoch, Paul Keating and Germaine Greer among his favourite detractors.

Monica Dux is a columnist with the *Age*, and the author of *Things I Didn't Expect (when I was expecting)* (2013), co-author of *The Great Feminist Denial* (2008), and editor of the anthology *Mothermorphosis* (2015). She can be heard regularly on ABC radio, and has published widely, especially on women's issues. Monica is one of the founders of the Stella Prize. You can find her at monicadux.com.au or on twitter @monicadux.

Roz Hammond is an actor and writer with credits that include five series of *Shaun Micallef's Mad as Hell*, *The Librarians*, *The Micallef P(r)ogram(me)*, *Muriel's Wedding* and *The Dish*. Her one-woman shows have toured internationally and been nominated for awards at the Melbourne International Comedy Festival and the Dublin Fringe Festival. Her television writing credits include *Eric*, *Small Tales and True*, *Skithouse*, *Home and Away*, *It's a Date* and *Little Lunch*.

Andrew Hansen is a member of comedy group The Chaser, whose TV shows include *Media Circus* (2014–15), *The Hamster Wheel* (2011–13), *The Chaser's War On Everything* (2006–9), and *CNNNN* (2002–3). As well as creating theatre shows, Andrew has made an ARIA-winning album, *The Blow Parade* (2010), and written for humorous newspaper *The Chaser* (1999–2005).

Lally Katz is one of the most produced Australian playwrights of her generation. Lally's original voice has won her multiple awards, commissions and fellowships, and continues to entertain audiences in Australia and internationally. Her show *Stories I Want to Tell You in Person* will be published as a memoir by Allen & Unwin in 2016.

Chris Leben is a writer, occasional actor, half-arsed comedian, director out of necessity and begrudging producer. He's currently the head comedy writer of *The Feed* on SBS2, and has a verified Twitter account and several TV shows in development that will probably never see the light of day.

Patrick Lenton is a blogger at *The Spontaneity Review* and the author of *A Man Made Entirely of Bats*. He is the recipient of the Thiel Grant for Online Writing, and was shortlisted for the 2014 Scribe Nonfiction Prize for Young Writers. He writes *The Rory Gilmore Reading Challenge*. He's a Digital Marketer at Momentum.

Lawrence Leung is an award-winning stand-up comedian, screenwriter and documentary maker best known for his geeky comedy and obsessive pursuits. He has hunted ghosts in Scottish castles on *Lawrence Leung's Unbelievable* (ABC1) and solved a Rubik's Cube whilst skydiving for *Choose Your Own Adventure* (ABC1). He managed not to have his head kicked in on ABC2's action/comedy series *Maximum Choppage*. His first feature film, *Sucker*, is adapted from Lawrence's award-winning one-man stage show of the same name. Lawrence is particularly chuffed because it stars Timothy Spall from the *Harry Potter* movies.

Tony Martin is a New Zealand-born comedian, writer and director based in Melbourne. His credits include *The D-Generation*, *The Late Show*, *Martin/Molloy*, *Get This* and *Upper Middle Bogan*. He is the author of three books and four angry letters to the *Age* 'Green Guide'.

Shaun Micallef is a TV comedian best known for *Talkin' 'Bout Your Generation* and *Shaun Micallef's Mad as Hell*. He is married with one wife, three children and a mortgage. He enjoys writing and has, so far, attempted three books: *Smithereens*, *Preincarnate* and *The President's Desk*.

Zoë Norton Lodge is a writer/presenter on *The Checkout* (ABC1) and a writer/panellist on *The Chaser's Media Circus* (ABC1). She is the co-creator of *Story Club,* a live, monthly storytelling night, TV show (ABC2) and podcast. She is thrilled to be sharing excerpts from her first book *Almost Sincerely* (Giramondo Publishing) in this anthology.

Liam Pieper's 2014 memoir, *The Feel-Good Hit of the Year*, follows his journey from starry-eyed flower child to inept gangster. It was shortlisted for the National Biography Award and the Ned Kelly Best True Crime Award, and widely praised for its honesty. His most recent book, *Mistakes Were Made*, is a volume of humorous essays that collectively make up a craven apology for being too honest in *Feel-Good Hit*.

Ben Pobjie is a comedian and author known for his television reviews, recaps and satirical pieces in publications including the *Age*, *Sydney Morning Herald*, *New Matilda*, *Crikey*, *The Roar* and others. He is also the author of *Surveying the Wreckage*, *The Book of Bloke* and *Superchef.* He lives in Melbourne with his wife, three children and growing inferiority complex.

Jane Rawson is the author of the novel, *A Wrong Turn at the Office of Unmade Lists*, which won the Small Press Network 2014 Most Underrated Book Award, and co-author of *The Handbook: Surviving and Living with Climate Change*, a practical, personal guide to life in a climate-changed Australia. Her novella, *Formaldehyde*, won the Seizure Viva La Novella Prize. Jane was formerly the Environment & Energy Editor for *The Conversation*, and her short fiction has been published by *Sleepers* and *Overland*.

Liam Ryan is a Melbourne-based comedian, writer and owner of ridiculous hair. He has gigged across Australia as a stand-up and improviser, and as part of award-winning sketch group WATSON. His comedy has been featured on the ABC and he also writes regularly for SBS Comedy. He has previously published gift books of questionable merit.

Luke Ryan is a Melbourne-based freelance writer and comedian, and author of the comic memoir *A Funny Thing Happened on the Way to Chemo*. His work has appeared in a number of publications including the *Guardian*, *Best Australian Essays*, *Smith Journal*, *The Lifted Brow*, *Junkee*, *Crikey*, *Kill Your Darlings* and many more. He also has a law degree, but would rather physically explode than use it.

Fiona Scott-Norman is a writer, comedian, DJ, cabaret director, dramaturg and teacher. Has no superannuation, and is currently reviewing her life choices. She has had three books published with Affirm Press (*50 Reasons to Quit Smoking*, *Don't Peak at High School* and *Bully For Them*), created two solo comedy shows (*The Needle and the Damage Done* and *Disco: The Vinyl Solution*), was a theatre and cabaret critic for the *Age*, and was raised with impeccable table manners.

Sami Shah is a comedian and writer who has been profiled in the *New York Times* and ABC's *Australian Story* and appeared on BBC Radio 4, BBC Asian Network, TEDx, *The Project*, the Soho Theatre, and *QI* with Stephen Fry. His autobiography, *I, Migrant*, has been nominated for the 2015 NSW Premier's Literary Award and the 2015 Russell Prize for Humour Writing. Sami produces a weekly podcast, *Sami Says*, writes columns for *SCOOP Magazine*, *Fairfax Media*, the *Courier-Mail* and many other publications, and is a frequent contributor on ABC720.

Rebecca Shaw (aka Brocklesnitch) is a freelance writer, podcaster and creator of the parody Twitter account @notofeminism. She is a columnist for *Kill Your Darlings*, is one of the team at The Backburner, and has written for SBS, *Junkee* and the *Guardian*. She is in constant competition with Ruby Rose to become Australia's favourite lesbian.

Robert Skinner worked for six years as a tour guide. He is the editor of a short-story magazine called *The Canary Press*.

Chris Taylor is a writer and performer who is best known as a member of The Chaser team, responsible for television programmes such as *The Chaser's War On Everything*, *CNNNN* and *The Hamster Wheel* on ABC. He now helps run the Giant Dwarf theatre venue in Sydney.

David Thorne is an Australian humourist, satirist, internet personality and author. His website, 27bslash6.com, receives several million hits per month, and his work has been featured on the BBC, *The Late Show with David Letterman*, *The Ellen DeGeneres Show* and *Late Night with*

Conan O'Brien. He exceeds others' tolerances, stays up too late and has offspring who thinks David doesn't know what he has been up to when he deletes his internet history.

Felicity Ward is a multi-award-winning Australian stand-up comedian, comic performer, writer and actor. She has written and toured numerous solo shows across Australia, Europe and the USA, and has appeared on many television shows including *Spicks and Specks*, *Thank God You're Here*, *Laid* and *Good News Week*. She has also appeared in the films *Any Questions for Ben?* and *The Inbetweeners 2*. In October 2014 she hosted the acclaimed ABC TV documentary *Felicity Ward's Mental Mission*, and her latest stand-up show, *What if There Is No Toilet*, premiered in Edinburgh last month.